Northumbrian Heritage

Also by Nancy Ridley

Portrait of Northumberland

Northumbrian Heritage

NANCY RIDLEY

Foreword by
Viscount Ridley

Illustrated

ROBERT HALE · LONDON

© *Nancy Ridley* 1968
First published in Great Britain November 1968
Reprinted February 1969
Reprinted October 1969

SBN 7091 0340 9

Robert Hale & Company
63 Old Brompton Road
London, S.W.7

Printed in Great Britain by
Lowe and Brydone (Printers) Ltd., London

Dedicated to the memory of my grandfather
Matthew Ridley of Peel Well

Contents

Illustrations

Illustrations

Map

ACKNOWLEDGEMENTS

Photographs are reproduced by courtesy of the following; No 5, 7, Lord Ridley; 6, Mr J. Browne-Swinburne; 1, 16, Barnaby's Picture Library; 2, 8, 9, 17, 20, Mr G. Douglas Bolton; 3, 4; 18, *Newcastle Chronicle and Journal;* 19 Mr Frank H. Meads; 12,13, *The Northumberland Gazette;* 22, Mrs H. Francis; remainder, the author.

Foreword

by Viscount Ridley

I am very glad to have the opportunity to write this foreword to Miss Nancy Ridley's book on Northumberland.

There is nobody who values the wealth of history in this county more than Miss Ridley. She has not forgotten what we all often forget, that history is still being made and descriptions such as this book gives will be of the greatest value to those future historians who will unearth their past which is our present.

She is also, like me, unrepentant provincial and in all her her pages she shares with her readers her love of this remote little-known even anachronistic corner of England and describes its life and its past with affection and reality.

I hope that it will be widely read and treasured by all who love Northumberland. I am particularly glad that a second reprint is needed so soon, showing the value of this excellent work.

Blagdon,
Northumberland

Ridley

Preface

This book is in no sense a sequel to my previous book, *Portrait of Northumberland*. The only similarity between the two is that, like its predecessor, this new book does not set out to be either a comprehensive history or a guide book.

Northumberland has so much history, and is such a vast county, that it was impossible to find room for a great deal of interesting material in *Portrait of Northumberland*. The only way to make it available to the large number of people, both in Northumberland and outside the county, who have expressed their wish to read more, is through another book. Two books have not of course sufficed to tell the complete story of this county of contrasts. Even the monumental 'County History' series has not yet achieved this end. As with my previous book the most difficult task has been to decide what to include and what to leave out—particularly onerous for one who admits to being a dedicated Northumbrian. I bitterly regret the many omissions which are inevitable.

Because of its geographical position Northumberland has not become a county inhabited by city dwellers; it is a county of vast expanse of open country, panoramic views and scenery of infinite variety. In the following pages I have tried to express how beautiful my county is. I have tried to include material which is representative of this border county and of the many places which lie between the Tyne and the Tweed. History and legend, folk songs and dialect, all have their place in Northumbrian Heritage.

It is incomprehensible to Northumbrians that their county, of which they are so proud, is one of the least known in the British Isles. In fact to the southerner who has never been north, the very name 'Northumberland' conjures up a picture of a bleak and barren land. This has deterred many people from seeing for themselves how wrong their impression is. When 'foreigners' do come to Northumberland the majority are soon converted, and become almost as voluble as Northumbrians in their praise of this most genuine of English counties. If this book in any way helps to dispel the misconceptions which many people have, then the time and labour spent in its creation will have been worthwhile.

I find it quite impossible to express in words my gratitude to the many people who have helped to make this book a reality. Each in their different way has made their contribution and without their help this book would never have been finished. I thank them all most sincerely.

Wylam,
Northumberland

N.R.

I

The Great North Road

I leave the drowsing South, and in thought I northward fly,
And walk the stretching moors that fringe the ever-calling sea,
    And am gladdened as the gales that are so bitter-sweet rush by,
While grey clouds sweetly darken o'er my North Countrie.
                                                —Thomas Runciman

THE most important road in Great Britain is the Great North
Road, better known to the majority of people as the A1, the link
between the capitals of England and Scotland, London and
Edinburgh. Nearly seventy miles of this famous road runs through
the County of Northumberland. Close to the seaboard in parts,
this road which has seen so much history, began as a rough track
which in Northumberland meandered for some of its journey
through the coastal plain, eventually forming a barrier between
industrial Northumberland to the east and the rich agricultural
areas which lie west of the road.

In the nineteenth century when the railways came, the London
to Edinburgh track followed closely the line of the road. This
revolution in transport superseded the coaches which up till
then carried passengers and freight between the two countries.
Now in the twentieth century the main road is a motor-way on
which many, in their desire for speed, miss so much of the beauty
of the old Northumbrian stretches of the 'old' Great North Road.

Many changes are taking place at the time of writing, and a new
road is under construction, but the A1 will still follow the
Pilgrim's route (after which Pilgrim Street is named). Some of
the villages are already by-passed, and there are a few miles of
dual carriageway.

By following the route of the old road, and branching off to both east and west, the visitor to Northumberland, can see unspoilt villages and scenery which so many people who dismiss this incomparably lovely county as dull, and merely the quickest way either to London or Scotland, never discover.

Once the boundaries of the City and County of Newcastle are left behind, and Northumberland begins, there is very little sign of industry. As far as Seaton Burn the road runs through a built-up area, and looking eastwards several pit-heaps can be seen. But by the time the roads to Bedlington and Ashington leave the North Road, and the entrance to Blagdon, the seat of Lord Ridley, is reached, the scenery which lies on either side is purely agricultural. No longer is this eastern triangle of Northumberland the great coal-field it was; many of the mines are redundant, and new towns such as Killingworth and Cramlington are attracting a different type of industry to the area, and bringing in 'foreigners' from other parts of the country.

The land through which the road marches on its way to the Border, has seen many changes since the days when it was merely a rough track through wild barren scenery. Later it became a rutted road, changing its course through the years, a road which English and Scottish armies traversed during the ceaseless warfare that raged until the Union of the Crowns. The coming of the stage and post coaches changed its character again, and many were the posting houses that were established along the highway. Time has lent romance—in many cases overrated—to the stage coaches. Tired horses and brutal coachmen were more realistic than all the colourful stories which have been handed down. The Christmas-card picture of the happy looking passengers descending at the Inn to be welcomed by a beaming mine host may have been true in some cases, but the poor, who could not afford a seat inside, and who had to put up with the rough accommodation provided for them, must have been thankful when their journey was over. The bitter east wind which blows off the North Sea in winter, to say nothing of the snow drifts, which still today block parts of the great highway, must have made the journey an ordeal for many. It is interesting to study old maps, and observe how the course of the road has changed so often that it is difficult to follow its precise original line.

When the days of the railway dawned there was opposition to its building from the great landlords; now there is opposition to the closure of so many railway stations which have served the people of Northumberland. Very few of the smaller stations are open now, and it is sad to see them neglected and derelict. At one time, not so long ago, many of the stations between Newcastle and Berwick were a blaze of flowers and won prizes for the best kept stations on the line. It is an anachronism that in this modern age there are several hand-operated level crossings on the line between Newcastle and Berwick.

Close to the coalfield are Plessey Woods through which the river Blyth flows. This part of the river is overlooked by Hartford Hall, now a Rehabilitation Centre for the disabled. Plessey Woods are a favourite picnic spot, as the banks of the river are thickly wooded.

A charming village to the east of the road is Hepscott, and although, due to its position so near to the ever-expanding town of Morpeth, many new houses have been built, it has not yet lost its rural character.

The even more delightful village of Bothal, with its castle dating from 1343 when the licence to crenellate was granted, is now a 'shop window' for a firm of manufacturers of electrical components, who have their factory at Bedlington. Bothal Castle is used to entertain guests, or potential customers of the firm. Surely the most hard-headed business tycoon must succumb to the charms of this village.

The traveller can return to the A1 south of Stannington by using a by-way. This village is divided into two parts by the new road. The old road can still be used, and this would probably be the road used by Doctor Johnson's familiar, James Boswell, who sometimes broke his journey at Morpeth when he was on his way to visit his brother then detained in a mental home in Newcastle. From Stannington, the road continues its course to Morpeth, which has the most delightful approach of all

B

Northumbrian towns. The steep slopes on the west side of the road are planted with flowers, while what was once an ugly rubbish tip is now an open space of turf dotted with trees. The most outstanding building as the traveller enters the town is what was at one time the County Gaol and now the Headquarters of the Morpeth Division of the Northumberland Constabulary. The gateway was designed by Dobson the Newcastle architect, in 1822, and great was the outcry from the ratepayers of those days that prisoners should have such imposing surroundings; Morpeth has now the largest population of any Northumbrian market town; its proximity to Newcastle (it is only fifteen miles away) has encouraged building contractors, and many are the housing estates on the outskirts of this historic town. Old buildings are being demolished in the name of progress, but Telford's famous nineteenth-century bridge will continue to carry the heavy traffic of the Great North Road. At present the road to the North goes through the centre of Morpeth, climbing steeply as it leaves the town behind.

Between Morpeth and the County Town of Alnwick, roads branch off the highway to the east and west. Many of these lead at first into the coal-field, but the scenery is not all marred by pit-heaps, and 'back-to-back' rows of pitmen's houses. Many of these have already been replaced by modern terraces and semi-detached houses. There are some delightful, surprisingly interesting, hamlets and villages in this industrial area, all of which is surrounded by the farmland which is the mainstay of the County.

It is in this part of Northumberland that Newcastle University has its Agricultural Research Station, Cockle Park, where there is a Pele Tower incorporated in the farm house. Cockle Park was once the property of the ancient family of Ogle, who are reputed to have been one of the proudest in the County. They had their chief seat at the little hamlet which still bears their name, and is situated about eleven miles north-west of Newcastle. The castle of this once famous family is part of a manor house, dating from the seventeenth century. A story has been handed down, that the Ogles had such a good opinion of themselves, that when the Dacres, a Cumberland family, claimed to be of older lineage, the

Ogles killed the Dacre's unfortunate supporter, who was, strangely enough, one of the Northumbrian Milburns.

The Ogle family had another tower in this part of the county. On the west side of the road to the Border, is the little hamlet of Causey Park. Here on the tower can be seen the arms of this proud race. The Tower now forms part of a house, and in the garden is a sundial, bearing an inscription, comparing the time at noon, at 'Cassapark' with other parts of Europe. The date is 1705. Long before the days of British Summer Time!

Not far from Cockle Park, and east of the road is the small hamlet of Hebron, which is of great antiquity. There is a little church, which was in such a condition in 1647, that a Doctor Basire reported it was "most scandalously and dangerously ruinous, under propt within with eight crutches, without with three; the seats all upturned or broken". According to *Life in Northumberland during the Sixteenth Century* by W. W. Tomlinson, this seems to have been the condition of most of the ecclesiastical buildings in the Northumberland of those wild days. In the next century Hebron was evidently still neglected by the clergy, and their undoubtedly lawless parishioners. To have once been the Cradle of Christianity, seems to have had little impact on the Northumbrians in the centuries that followed.

It was not only the highwaymen who contributed to tales of dark deeds on the Great North Road. Long before their time the lawless Northumbrians committed countless barbarous deeds. Two families who had their homes between Morpeth and Felton, the Herons and the Lisles, hated one another bitterly. Having had one of their many arguments, a Heron fled to the nearest church for sanctuary, but Lisle, his pursuer, caught him and killed him in the church porch. The people of nearby Brockenfield, then a large village, captured the murderer and cut off his head in a nearby dene, bearing the unusual name of Kitswell. On this part of the road there was a diversion by Helm, to avoid a long climb for the coach horses.

At Eshott, the home of Mr T. P. H. Sanderson, is the famous Ayrshire herd of cattle, the first pedigree herd of this breed to be established south of the Border. In the disastrous outbreak of foot-and-mouth disease from which Northumberland suffered so terribly in the summer of 1966, part of this famous herd had to be destroyed, but mercifully some of the stock escaped.

The minor roads which lead towards the coast are now free from signs of industry; the end of the industrial triangle is at the port of Amble. To the west the roads make their way through farming country towards the hills, magnificent views of Simonside and Cheviot now forming the background of Northumberland. The road which has seen so much history winds its way to Felton, dropping down to this village which has its setting on both banks of the Coquet, which is crossed there by a stone bridge. This village, which is a favourite haunt of fishermen, is most attractive especially where the houses stand on the west bank of the river. Here the 'big' house is Felton Park, where legend says the Jacobites stabled their horses in the 'Fifteen'. If this is true, the pitiful little army would have crossed the existing bridge, which is medieval. If the coaches used this route, the pull up out of Felton must have been a great strain for the horses.

The village church is dedicated to St Michael; it has been altered so many times, that it is a puzzle even to antiquarians. At old Felton there was once a village destroyed by that most insufferable king, John, who did so much damage in the county. John's ambition in life seems to have been to destroy his kingdom.

North of Felton a road leads eastwards to Warkworth, and by deviating the traveller comes to one of the most attractive places in the county, Guyzance, with a ruined chapel standing in a field by the banks of the Coquet. This chapel was dedicated to St Wilfrid, but comparatively little has been written about its history; in fact very little seems to be known. A directory of Northumberland for 1855 says that the chapel was given to the monks of Alnwick Abbey by Eustace Fitzjohn, but though Tanner's Monastica gives the information that the chapel was endowed with the tithes and two bovates of land, there are no other records of its history. The banks of the river are lined with trees, the houses are sturdy and stone built, and at one time there was a mill, marked on the ordnance map as Walkmill. Guyzance has its big house too, owned by the Milburn family. In 1855 the village had its blacksmith and agricultural implement maker; a joiner, a schoolmaster, a miller of course, a shop-keeper and a George Tate, described as a yeoman who lived at East House. In 1831 there was a population of 213 'souls'. With the ever increasing drift from the land Guyzance cannot boast of so many 'souls' in 1968. Guyzance is close to the busy A.1. with its endless stream of traffic, yet its atmosphere is so peaceful.

There is a curious anecdote associated with the building of a weir at Acklington in 1776-8; the salmon which have made Coquet one of the most famous fishing rivers in the country were unable to get over the weir. A Mr Buckland was one day watching the vain attempts of the fish, and being filled with pity for them, promised the fish that as the Duke of Northumberland was a kind man he was quite sure that His Grace would have a ladder made for them: Mr Buckland must have been a most extraordinary man, as he put up a notice on the weir which read as follows:

Notice To Salmon And All Bull Trout.
    No road at present over this weir. Go down stream, taking the first turn to the right, and you will find good travelling water up stream, and no jumping required. F.T.B.

It would be fascinating to know if the Duke was approached, and what His Grace's reactions were. At Acklington where the weir was built, there was a Fighter Command Station during the Second World War which was operational until 1969.

Before the dual carriageway begins, and strangely enough there are very few such on the Northumbrian stretch of the country's most famous road, there stands on the west side of the verge a stone obelisk, in sadly neglected surroundings. This monument has an unusual history. In the late eighteenth and early nineteenth centuries there lived at Swarland Hall, a house which is now demolished, a Mr Alexander Davison, who was a victualler to the Admiralty during the Napoleonic wars. In 1807 this gentleman erected the obelisk, in front of his home at Swarland. The inscription reads: "Not to commemorate the Public Virtues and Heroic Achievements of Nelson, which is the duty of England, but to the Memory of Private Friendship, this erection is dedicated by Alexander Davison". The inference is that the owner of Swarland was extremely proud of his friendship with England's greatest Admiral. When Swarland was demolished in this century, the monument was removed to its present position. A mile north of the monument is Newton Hall, the property of the ancient family of Widdrington. A Samuel Widdrington married Davison's daughter, Dorothy; hence the obelisk's present site.

Climbing steadily the 'old' road passes the gates of the Hall on its way to the village of Newton-on-the-Moor, from which there is a magnificent view of the incomparable Northumbrian coastline. Newton Hall was originally an Elizabethan farmhouse, to which additions have been made in the course of time. Abandoned by the family in 1931, it was during the last war used as a school, and later 'occupied' by the Army, when sad to say, a great deal of damage was done. Now Newton Hall is again the home of a Widdrington, Captain Francis Widdrington, who was High Sheriff of his county in 1966. The house is approached by a long drive, and stands in delightful gardens, especially the south-east garden, with its yew hedges and ha-ha. The house is entered by a long conservatory, which was designed by a member of the family to prevent any visitor from catching him in the garden unannounced! Now this conservatory which was once an orangery, is filled with flowering plants which are a mass of colour.

The dining table is of interest as it was a gift from Lord Nelson to Alexander Davison, and is of West Indian mahogany. The beautiful break-front book-case in the library was specially made for the house in the eighteenth century. The ornate stuccoed ceilings are the work of the same Italian artists who were employed by the fourth Duke of Northumberland to produce the magnificent work at Alnwick. Newton Hall claims to be the first house in Northumberland where a form of central heating was installed, and this is still functioning today. Perhaps it was Shalcross Fitzherbert Widdrington, the present owner's grandfather, who was such an ardent admirer of Italy and all things Italian, that he felt something must be done to combat the cold of the long

Northumbrian winters. The Italian murals are a memorial to this descendant of the Widdrington who helped to make Northumbrian history. The name will ever be remembered when the Battle of Otterburn is mentioned, as it was there a Widdrington fought on after both his legs had been severed. In this Border county that has seen so much bloodshed and strife, now there is peace; and Newton Hall is left behind in its seclusion, surrounded by farmlands, where cattle are no longer 'lifted' and the sheep graze safely. The traffic of the Great North Road by-passes this pleasant house, and the road goes on towards the ducal town of Alnwick. In the village of Newton-on-the-Moor is the strangely named Cook and Barker Inn, the origin of which is problematical.

North towards Alnwick marches the road where the traffic at present passes through the archway of the Hotspur Gate. Some time ago there was a threat to 'develop' this ancient town; happily this is not to be carried out. The people of Alnwick protested so vociferously against this sacrilege, that for once the planners were defeated. The name of Alnwick is synonymous with the great house of Percy, and the castle which has been their fortress home for generations.

Many are the pleasant villages which are close to the major road. Denwick, which is a mile to the east, on a side road which leads to Longhoughton and the coast, has interesting connections with a family named Common, who lived there in the nineteenth century, and who performed the most extraordinary feats. In fact Mr John Common, who invented a double drill turnip sower, would seem to have been the only normal member of this eccentric family. For his invention, John was recognized by the Society of Arts, and presented with a silver medal and ten guineas. It seems rather unusual for the Arts to be interested in agricultural implements! The Highland Society, now the Royal Highland Agricultural Society of Scotland, were not to be outdone by the Arts, and gave Mr Common thirty guineas. History records that the Commons were remarkable for their strength, stature, longevity and cleverness. The great-grandfather of the inventor is reputed to have achieved the age of a hundred and ten, and that shortly before his death "nature endowed him with a new set of teeth". This strange character left seven sons, one of whom used to walk from Thrunton, a distance of several miles, with a bolt of peas suspended from his shoulders. (A bolt was an old measure. Presumably this is the same as a boll, which at Alnwick consisted of six bushels of barley or oats—as opposed to Hexham, where the boll consisted of five bushels.) Robert Common was employed at the farm of Warkworth Barns, where he threw into the river two men who had insulted his master. This Robert enjoyed giving demonstrations of his strength, and once at High Buston, near Alnmouth, he tossed an axe over a house. The next generation of the family, whose exploits must have vastly entertained the district, were even more peculiar. One son was, not surprisingly, reprimanded by his father for standing on his head on the steeple of Shilbottle church! The records do not say what punishment was meted out to another John Common who also indulged in this curious pastime, though in this case he stood on his head on the highest tower of Warkworth Castle, the Percy stronghold where the Champion of Northumberland, Harry Hotspur, lived. The Percy achieved his place in history as a 'bonnie' fighter, while Mr Common is remembered for his climbing activities, as he went from Warkworth to the Brizlee Tower in Hulne Park, where he again performed his dangerous act. The County of Northumberland has produced some extraordinary people, but surely none stranger than the Commons.

In the neighbourhood of Denwick, at Ratcheugh Crags, is an observatory built by the first Duke of Northumberland to designs by Robert Adam, who also was responsible for the Brizlee Tower. Here on this out-crop of Whin-Sill the observatory commands glorious views of sea, hills and the rich grazing land of which there is so much in this part of Northumberland. According to records at Alnwick, this rather incongruous looking building dates from about 1780. It consists of one room with windows on all sides, which was used by the Duke's family when they rode to the coast by the Green Lane, which stretched from the Castle to Boulmer. Part of the observatory is a small cottage which at one time housed a game-keeper; now it is let as an ordinary cottage.

Here at Ratcheugh is held the Point-to-Point Meeting of the Percy Hunt, of which the present Duke of Northumberland is Master. This course has one of the most attractive settings for racing in the county. In 1966, when the Meeting was held in April, the sun blazed from a cloudless sky, the North Sea was the colour of the Mediterranean. Combined with the 'colours' of the riders as they raced round this perfect course, it made an unforgettable picture, not only for those who enjoy scenery, but for those who love steeplechasing. This Point-to-Point is a combination of three Northumbrian Hunts, The Percy, West Percy, and Milvain.

Returning to the main road which leaves the County Town, at the point where the dangerous Lion Bridge crosses over the river Aln. This bridge has many times been damaged by the ever increasing amount of traffic. The line of the road to the Border will soon follow yet another of the many changes of route which have so often happened in its long history; extensive road alterations are now being made.

From Alnwick to Belford, once described by Cobbett in his *Rural Rides* as waste land, is now well wooded, and perhaps the most attractive stretch of the Great North Road within Northumberland. It was on this part of their journey that the coaches so often met with disaster. Charlton Mires, five miles north of Alnwick, is so named because the coaches were so often stuck in the mire. Before this once notorious danger spot is reached, and halfway between Alnwick and Charlton Mires, are the ruins of a Pele tower which was used as a look-out by the Percys, in the days when all Northumbrians lived dangerously. The spelling of the tower's name varies considerably from Hefferlaw, Highfarlaw to Heffordlaw. Certainly the 'high' is appropriate as the road climbs steeply all the way from Alnwick.

The Kyloe Hills now appear to the north-west where they form a background for the small town of Belford. Today Belford is a pleasant place, with its Market Cross and its long low inn, the Blue Bell, once a famous coaching house. Belford apparently was not always the civilized place it is today, as a certain Mr Rawdon, who came to it in the seventeenth century describes it as "a miserable beggarly sodden town, or town of sods. In all the town not a loaf of bread, nor a quart of beer, nor a lock of hay, nor a peck of oats, and little shelter for horse or man". Poor Mr Rawdon must have been thankful to leave such an inhospitable place. Could he come back now he would receive a very different reception at the Blue Bell. Driving on this stretch of the road is as hazardous today as in the hey-day of the coach, though in a different way. The road south of Belford is a series of sharp bends, and here there have been many fatal accidents. Belford has a Live Stock Mart to which buyers come from all over the country.

Buckton, a little hamlet further north, was the scene of a most daring exploit in July 1685, when a Scottish girl, Grizel Cochrane, held up The London Mail at the point of a pistol, and seized her father's death warrant. A clump of trees, Grizie's Clump is reputed to be the spot where this intrepid girl carried out her plan so successfully, and thereby saved her father's life. Naturally such an exploit inspired the ballad mongers, and Sir John Cochrane's escape from death, due to the courage and determination of his daughter, is described in verse:

> The warlocks are dancing threesome reels,
> On Goswick's haunted links;
> The red fire shoots by Ladythorne,
> And Tam wi' the lantern falls and sinks.
> On Kyloe hills there's awfu' sounds,
> But they frightened not Cochrane's Grizzy,
> The moonbeams shot from the troubled sky,
> In glints of flickerin' light;
> The horseman came skelping thro' the mire,
> For his mind was in fright.
> His pistol cocked he held in his hand,
> But the feint a fear had Grizzy.
> As he came fornenst the Fenwicke woods,
> From the whin bushes shot out a flame;
> His dappled filly reared up in affright,
> And backward over he came.
> There's a hand on his craig, and a foot on his mouth,
> 'Twas Cochrane's bonny Grizzy.
> "I will not take thy life", she said,

"But gie me thy London news;
No blood of thine shall fyle my blade,
Gin me ye dinna' refuse."
She's prie'd the warrant and away she flew,
With the speed and strength of the wild curlew.

The events which led up to this 18-year-old girl's melodramatic deliverance of her father, were that he had been involved in the Rising of The Duke of Argyll, in the early part of the unhappy reign of James II and VII. Sentenced to death, Cochrane of Ochiltree was in the Tolbooth Prison in Edinburgh. Hopes of a reprieve were entertained, as bribes had been supplied by the Earl of Dundonald, who was Sir John's father. Nevertheless Grizel was determined to take no chances, and so she crossed the Border and stayed with her old nurse. Disguising herself as a man she went to a public house near Belford where the postman stayed, and while the man was sleeping she stole his pistols. The ghost of Grizel Cochrane is still said to haunt the scene of her triumph.

On the west side of the road is the hamlet of Fenwick (not to be confused with another Fenwick near Stamfordham, in the south of the county). The Fenwick Women's Institute hold their meetings in what has once been a granary, which is reached by an outside flight of stone steps. The road is now running closer to the sea as it nears the end of its Northumbrian journey. On either side are the huge farms of North Northumberland; that at Beal, where the travellers cross the causeway to Holy Island, is 1,040 acres. The present house was built in 1674. The most outstanding landmark on the way to Berwick on the Tweed is the tall gaunt tower of Haggerston Castle, with a large dove-cote resembling what the French call a *colombière*.

Grizel Cochrane's ghost is not the only supernatural visitor to this lovely corner of Northumberland. On Lowick Moor at midnight, a being known as the Lady of Barmoor transforms herself into a white hare. Why she comes from her own moor to Lowick legend does not say. Scott mentions Barmoor Ridge in *Marmion*.

Scotland is now very near and the journey is reaching its end, as the red roofs of Berwick appear on the north bank of the lovely river Tweed. At Tweedmouth, the river ends its course from Scotland, to which Berwick was known as 'The Key'. Berwick with its commanding position, its wonderful Elizabethan walls, its bridges and its history, is the last town in Northumberland on this East Coast route to the Border which ends at Lamberton Toll.

To those people who are not familiar with the vagaries of this Border town, it must be most confusing to cross the Border into the County of Berwickshire, yet the Town of Berwick is in Northumberland! Here are the steep red sandstone cliffs which stand like sentinels as the North Sea breaks against them.

Nearly seventy miles of Northumberland's share of the Great North Road has come to its end. The signs appear, England; Scotland, and the two countries which waged ceaseless warfare for the possession of the Port of Berwick, meet, and now are at peace. The crossing of the Border into Berwickshire lacks the dramatic setting of the Carter Bar, but the road is certainly the most famous and historic of all. From a track through wasteland, it has changed its character with the passing of time; but it can never in its long history be described as a peaceful road. A more appropriate name would be the Restless Road. A fitting epitaph for A1. might be a line from the late Sir Harry Lauder's famous song "Keep Right On To The End Of The Road":

> With a good stout heart for a long steep hill,
> You will get there in the end.

2

The Northumbrian Speech

MY CANNY HINNY
Where hes te been, my canny hinny?
An' where hes te been, my bonny bairn?
Aw was up an' doon, seekin' my hinny;
Aw was throo' the toon, seekin' for my bairn.
—From *Songs of Northern England*

FOR many years the writer has threatened to compile a phrase book of the Northumbrian speech for the guidance of 'foreigners' who come to Northumberland for the first time. The term 'foreigner' does not mean visitors from overseas, but people from other parts of the United Kingdom who have not been fortunate enough to be born in the most beautiful and historic county in the British Isles. The language of Northumberland is one of the most difficult of all provincial dialects to understand and every sympathy is felt for those who have no knowledge of its peculiarities.

This attempt to convey its many variations is no scholarly treatise, nor is it a glossary, but a collection of words, idioms, and sayings, some still in common use and others, as traditions die out, now only to be found in the pages of local history books.

It is a peculiar characteristic of the British character that when with the march of progress traditions and customs die, every effort is made to preserve them. This is certainly the case with dialects. More interest is being taken in regional speech than ever before, not only in the northern counties of England, but in the southern counties and in Scotland.

Some years ago Edinburgh University circulated a questionnaire throughout Northumberland, stating quite rightly that we have a tongue in both countries, although the intonation is different. The object of this survey was to ascertain how many dialect words are still used, whether in the towns or the country districts, by old or young people, and asking for examples of dialect words such as doorlatch, which in Northumberland is a *sneck*. Another dialect survey was recently carried out by Professor Orton, then of Leeds University, and recordings were made. Professor Orton's survey was made in collaboration with P. Halliday and the late Professor Dieth of Zürich.

Brockett's Glossary of North Country Words with their Etymology and Affinity to other languages and occasional Notices of Local Customs and Popular Superstitions in two volumes, is of great value to those interested in the subject. This book, compiled in the last century, was revised by Brockett's son, a solicitor in Newcastle, although a Durham man. An F.S.A., John Trotter Brockett was born at Witton Gilbert (the *G* is given the soft pronunciation) in the County of Durham, and lived for many years in Gateshead. At one time this lover of North Country speech was Secretary of the Newcastle Literary and Philosophical Society. The original manuscript of this now priceless Glossary was bought by the then Earl of Durham for 8 guineas; today it is practically impossible to find a second-hand copy of the printed book. Brockett's memorial is the research and material he left for future generations.

In the 1890s the English Dialect Society published *A Glossary of Words Used in The County of Northumberland and on Tyneside*. In two volumes by Richard Oliver Heslop; complete with a map of Northumberland, dividing the districts according to the variations of speech. This Glossary has now become a classic. No doubt Heslop owed a great deal to his predecessor Brockett; in fact he pays tribute to him. Unfortunately few derivations are given, and there is a great deal of disagreement and supposition regarding the origins: nevertheless everyone interested in the Northumbrian speech must study these two volumes by Heslop.

Britain has so often been invaded in the past and, although people are inclined to forget this fact, has on many occasions been an 'occupied country'. Settlers have left a heritage of words, which have been Anglicized, or in the case of Northumberland, 'Northumbrianized'. The Northumbrian is an expert when it comes to distorting, not only pronunciation but grammar too. It is a waste of time to point out to a true native of the county that he or she may be wrong, as in their own estimation the Northumbrian is never *wrang*; it's always the other man who doesn't know any better. Until the Compulsory Education Act of 1870, a great number of people were unable to read or write and used pronunciations they heard from their parents and grandparents; woe betide them if they were Northumbrians.

Even today teachers, especially in the colliery districts, find it extremely difficult to teach the children to spell correctly, as they spell the words as they have heard them pronounced. Northumberland, due to its rather isolated position on the map retains more dialect speech than the more accessible counties, and the majority of the people, whatever their station in life (if one dare use that expression today), are bi-lingual. The writer is only proficient in one 'foreign language' and that is the speech of her own county. Until the turn of the century very few people travelled as they do today; they were born, brought up and died in their isolated villages. Now, with the movement of the population from one part of the country to another (especially in the case of the miners who are redundant, and have to emigrate to find work), the dialect and intonation will change, and the enormous influence of radio and television all have their effect.

The ideal is to be able to speak standard English and yet to be familiar with the local speech. The Northumbrian tongue is unintelligible to others, and this has been proved when attempts have been made to put on a play, in either Tyneside or Northumbrian. In London, Yorkshire, Lancashire, stage Irish and Scots are accepted, but 'wor tongue has them bested'.

Some etymologists claim that intonation is the result of the geographical situation of the district, and that in the hilly mountainous parts of the country there a is lilt in the voice. This is certainly true of the Highlands and Western Isles of Scotland, where the most musical and attractive voices in Great Britain are to be heard. Northumberland on the other hand has a sing-song intonation impossible to convey. The voice is raised at the end of every sentence and falling inflections are never used. This, especially on Tyneside is monotonous, as very little emphasis is introduced, whether the speaker is recounting good news or bad.

The stranger to this Border county is often under the misapprehension that Northumberland and its speech is all Tyneside, and designates the inhabitants as 'Geordies'. This applies only to the industrial area and overpopulated Tyneside. The rest of Northumberland is one of the most sparsely populated counties in England, and the speech is rural as distinct from the loud raucous language of the industrial areas.

The manner in which the people earn their living has a bearing on their manner of speech. The fisher folk have their own expressions and words; the miners, and the farmers, although with the spread of mechanization in agriculture, technical terms are superseding the old words.

The distinctive 'French' R is heard throughout the county except in Allendale, which, lying so close to the Cumberland Border, uses the trilled consonant. No satisfactory explanation has ever been given why this peculiar R is heard only in Northumberland. It may be a relic from some long ago invaders, or the popular legend that it sprang from the most famous member of the House of Percy, Harry, known as Hostpur, who, it is said, had a speech defect and that the Northumbrians of his day imitated their hero. When *Henry IV* was broadcast, the actor who played the part of Northumberland's hero made an attempt to produce the local pronunciation, but not with great success. Only someone born in the county is capable of producing the Hotspur R.

In spite of the many books which have been written on the subject of regional speech and the many theories propounded, it is remarkable that in such a small nation there are so many variations; perhaps the Tower of Babel is the answer.

It could be said that there are three different languages in Northumberland with many subdivisions, Tyneside, Pitmatic and Rural.

Morpeth, the town on the Wansbeck

Tyneside is the language of the Geordies, which to be honest, is something of a mongrel. Final consonants are discarded, and the Geordie speaks so rapidly that it is difficult, even for natives of other parts of the county, to keep pace with whatever is being said. It has been suggested that the loud voice, as opposed to the softer utterance of the countryman, is the outcome of working in the noisy factories and ship-yards. A short *A* is used generally, and the Tynesider pronounces Newcastle as Newcassel. Unlike in other parts of England the *H* is always sounded, nor is it ever added in the wrong place.

Many songs have been written in the Tyneside tongue, and it is regrettable that attempts have been made by the more 'refained' to Anglicize such famous songs as Tyneside's national anthem 'Blaydon Races'. Sung in English these traditional songs lose their meaning, as it is in the familiar dialect that their appeal lies, especially to exiles. 'Keep yer feet still, Geordie Hinny' would never be the same without the dialect words, and the famous 'Wor Nanny's a Mazer', though to be accurate, the scene of Nanny's exploits was south of the Tyne, at Rowlands Gill in the adjoining county of Durham.

'Hinny' once so commonly used to denote a term of endearment, and is no doubt a corruption of honey, as being sweet, is now replaced by less pleasant terms, such as 'luv' and 'pet' which are not indigenous to the county, nor are they pleasant to hear. 'Hinny' is a kindly word, and its disappearance is to be deplored.

The speech of the Northumbrian miner could be described as 'Pitmatic', and is very difficult to understand, as the average miner dispenses with articulation and speaks out of the side of his mouth, with many nods of his 'heid', aye's and queer guttural sounds.

The pronoun, so largely used, presents another problem to the uninitiated, very seldom does a miner's wife refer to her husband by his christian name, 'He gan's in' or the broader 'Wors' meaning ours. Every member of the family is communal property and members are addressed as 'Our so and so'.

'In-bye' and 'Out-bye' are terms referring to the position of

C

the coal-seams in relation to their distance from the shaft in which the men are working. These terms strangely enough are used in the agricultural districts also to denote hill or lowland farms. When a colliery stops working it is 'idle', so is a mischievous child. Many of the expressions that appear to be ridiculous have their origin in the mists of time. 'Sittin' on his hunkers' as pitmen do, is from the Icelandic, haunches, and in low seams he is literally on his hunkers. In the days of the old pit rows (Seghill can boast of the most delightful name of them all, 'Spicecake Row') the men crouched on their hunkers outside the cottage doors, often with their whippets beside them while a Stotty Cake cooled on the window sill. The recipe is as follows: dough as for bread and allow to rise; cut off about 1 lb; flatten out and place on baking tin; Bake until brown, turn and brown on other side; eat whilst fresh.

Where pit ponies are used they are known as 'Galloways', and in the Morpeth district in times gone by the miners were paid fortnightly, and the Friday between pay days was called 'baff' Friday. The greeting 'What fettle?' is derived from Anglo-Saxon, otherwise 'How are you?' 'What cheer?' is another common form of greeting between 'marrers' or friends, who are the mates with whom a miner works. 'Marrers' is also used in the sense of likeness or similarity, and to describe someone of outstanding ability: 'We'll never see his marrer (equal) again.'

There are several purely pitmatic terms for illness. 'A'hs not varry cliver' interpreted is 'I'm not very well'. 'A'hs champion'—I'm better; 'Yor luking gey shabby'—looking ill; and 'Gey hard up' does not apply to money but to a severe illnesss.

In the rural parts of the county there are also many peculiar references to illness, as the Northumbrian is nothing if not dramatic when it comes to describing how someone 'Took bad', 'Had a badly bout', 'Took to his bed' and 'Is a lang way through' meaning that there is little hope of recovery. To die is to 'Get away' and no matter what the age of the sufferer, or the length of the illness, Northumbrians always 'Get away sharp'. Although funerals have ceased to be the spectacular displays of days gone by, when the colliery bands accompanied the cortège, the popularity of the dear departed is still expressed by the number of mourners, and 'What a cars'.

It is impossible to determine how many variations there are in the country districts beyond the industrial area of the coalfield. The vowel sounds change from one village to another, home on Tyneside is 'hyem', at Hexham it is 'heam', and the Border 'gans hame'.

'Canny' is one of the most frequently used words, and in many different contexts; it expresses fondness for someone, a warning to be careful. Distance is 'A canny way'; the amount of rain that has fallen 'A canny sup' and it describes anyone who is careful with their money. Newcastle is described as 'Canny Newcassel, the pride of the North'. A word in general use for mud and pools of water is 'clarts' and 'clarty'; unfortunately the etymology is unknown. The onomatopeic sound for clarts expresses so clearly its meaning. 'Ah was plodging (wading) through the clarts up to me oxters (arm-pits)'. One of the most delightful of these onomatopaeic words is 'Hap', to cover up; it has such a kindly sound. To 'Skelp a whinging bairn' again so expressive, is literally Gaelic to smack, whinging old German to mourn, and bairn Anglo-Saxon to bear.

The intonations of South and North Tynedale are entirely different, South Tyne is less musical, while the inhabitants of the North Tyne Valley purse their lips and the results are 'refained' sounds, which have to be heard to be appreciated. In the language of both valleys the hens are 'barred up' at nights, and the cattle are brought into the 'house' for the winter. North Tyne is the land of tea-pot spoots, and skorts, and the pronunciation of shirt, the old word for which now seldom heard was a sark, varies throughout the county. A broody hen is a clocker, from Anglo-Saxon to cluck, and this applies to the whole county, while birds are ploated instead of plucked, and when there is a heavy snow-fall the country people say 'The old woman is ploating her geese'.

The most musical of all Northumbrian speech in the writer's opinion is that of Coquetdale; it is soft and kindly, in keeping with the green land through which Coquet flows. In the Alnwick district and its many charming villages speech is slow with a strongly produced R, bearing out the legend of Hotspur. Where the great range of the Cheviots penetrates far into Northumberland the speech becomes more Scottish, and on a cold day, 'It's gey snell comin' doon the brae.'

Berwick and Tweedside is a mixture of both tongues, as befits the Border line. People do not live in Berwick they 'bide', while in other parts of the county they 'stop'. As well, becomes foreby, turnips become neeps (they are bagies near the coast). Several of the words have originated from the French language, no doubt because of the Auld Alliance that Scotland once had with France. A side dish in Northumberland is an ashette, a gooseberry a grozer, and to be 'dowly', that is to be sad and depressed, is obviously of French extraction.

The speech of the inhabitants of Holy Island is beyond even that of a born and bred Northumbrian, and is impossible to translate. Joined to the mainland only by a causeway, this island could be a foreign land. To appreciate this most involved of languages, the visitor interested in dialect must spend a holiday on the island.

All over the county people meet to have a 'crack' from the German *kracken*. 'Give us yor crack' is a familiar greeting, and if friends have not met for some time, the classic expression is, 'It's a gey lang time sin Ah clapped eyes on yer'. The Northumbrian changes the meaning of words indiscriminately, a bonny woman is a pretty one, but a bonny gliff is a nasty fright. 'Gliff' is probably derived from the German, as is 'dunch' (to collide, or nudge). Daft is from Scandinavian to be silly, but why daft as a brush. Fond is also used in the same sense.

Courting couples are described as 'nebbin' on', while when children 'stot' and 'kep' a ball, they are using Scandinavian words, to bounce and to catch. Anything that is sticky is 'claggy' from the Danish. To ken, as in Scottish, is to know. A dust is a 'stour', and a 'sackless' person is one lacking in common sense. In Heslop's Dictionary there are more than six hundred words which have at one time been used in Northumberland.

Had one the time and opportunity how interesting it would be to trace how many are used today, but as this chapter merely skims the surface of this fascinating subject, the reader is recommended to study Richard Heslop and his predecessor Brockett. No doubt some of the statements made in this brief survey will lead to controversy and argument, and the writer would never claim to be an authority—merely one who is intensely interested in the speech of her fellow Northumbrians, and who is thankful that she can speak and understand it, apart of course from Holy Island!

A peculiarity is that broth is referred to as 'a few' never some, and meals are always spoken of in the plural, dinners, teas and baits. A bilberry is a bleaberry, and an apple core a 'gowk', so is a senseless person, meaning useless, 'He's nobbut a gowk'. A turkey Jock becomes a 'Bubbly Jock', and to cry is either to bubble or greet, depending in which part of the county it is used. To be 'crouse' is to be pleased with one's self. To have a 'fozy' heid in the morning, means soft, from the Teutonic, spongy. A dovecote is a 'duckett', a sparrow a 'spuggy', and a donkey of course, a 'cuddy'.

Anyone who propounds theories on the origin of dialect words is open to criticism, as this letter from R. Oliver Heslop shows:

12 Akenside Hill,
Newcastle upon Tyne.
Dec. 3rd, 1888.

Rd. Oliver Heslop.

Telegraph. Heslop. Newcastle upon Tyne.
Telephone 430. Post Office.

Dear Mr Mackey,

I duly proposed you for membership [for what the writer does not say] at least such is my strong impression. The administration of the Society is a trifle slack in these matters and yours is not the first case I have heard of where the Society has omitted to advise that an election has taken place. I may have handed the proposal to the seconder to give in and between the two it may have gone adrift. However I at once wrote to the Secretary and I shall see that you are duly and truly installed.

Part one has been sold for as much as 20s. It is almost unobtainable,

The Rev. Low's was the last set I heard of. You might ask the Rev. Canon Greenwell where you are likely to get hold of it, or perhaps Stack of Durham might get hold of one.

Thanks for your kindly and much valued criticism on my works. No doubt I have in a few cases given too many examples. One is in nearly every case sufficient but there are sometimes varying shades of meaning to be illustrated and each one may then be amplified with advantage. I have tried to stick to this rule but I have purposely broken it in such words as 'Canny' for instance, where one cannot help being exuberant.

In some other cases of words commonly considered Scottish only have I been tempted to show that there is more than an isolated instance of their use, and therefore a warrant for including them in Northd. words. Please do not fail to tell me from time to time any other point that strikes you. I am truly grateful for your kind censorship.

With kind regards,
Faithfully Yours
R. Oliver Heslop.

Richard Oliver Heslop though a Novocastrian by birth was of Cumbrian parentage. Born in 1842, he became a successful iron and steel merchant, and died in Newcastle during the First World War.

Our Mr Heslop was lavish in his praise of other writers, and another letter written from Eskdale Terrace in 1903 to a Mr Boag is to congratulate him on an article in *The Westminster Gazette*, but this prolific writer and collector of Northumbrian words, does not state what Mr Boag's article was about! Years must have been spent in research, and no detail omitted; one cannot help wishing that as much time could be spent nowadays on this controversial subject.

In Heslop's day there was more leisure to indulge in what to him was truly a labour of love. The stranger to Northumberland has to contend too with the local pronunciations of place names, which bear no relation to the spelling. Villages such as Ovingham, Whittingham, and the town of Bellingham are all pronounced with the 'jum' sound peculiar to the county. The only omission is the famous Chillingham of the Wild White Cattle, which is too much of a tongue twister even for a Northumbrian. Ulgham near Morpeth becomes Uffham, Alnham in the vale of Whittingham, is Yeldham, and Alwinton is Allenton, to quote only a few examples of traps for the unwary. A map is no help to the traveller, to ask for Humsha' as the stranger pronounces Humshalf (Humshaugh) in North Tynedale makes a native 'bad with laffin' '.

Shopping for household goods also presents a problem. A large kitchen knife is a 'gully', a griddle a 'girdle', at one time a wooden spoon used for stirring porridge was a 'thivel', and was also used to make a 'hasty pudding', which is a traditional dish made from boiling milk, flour or oatmeal—or both, seasoned with salt, and cold milk added. In his *Journal* Daniel Defoe records that at Felton on the Great North Road between Morpeth and Alnwick he was 'regaled' with hasty pudding. Bread and hot milk sometimes flavoured with sugar and nutmeg is 'boiley' and is regarded as a suitable dish for invalids. A 'hot crowdie' is composed of oatmeal and hot fat from the joint and seasoned to taste. The joints of meat vary in parts of the county; there are no half shoulders of lamb or mutton in Coquetdale, as in Scotland they are quarters.

Those engaged in agriculture, whether they be Northumbrians or not, are usually bi-lingual, and certainly it is an advantage to be able to give instructions to the sheep dogs and horses in the vernacular. The countless collie dogs of Northumberland with their monosyllabic names would ignore the English 'Get Behind', but Moss, Tyne and Tweed readily answer to 'Get back in a hint lad'. A pig sty becomes a pig 'cree', the hens sit on 'bokes' (perches), an odd man, one who does general farm work is a 'loose man' in the south of the county and 'An 'orra man' where Northumberland marches with the Scottish Border.

A kitten is known as a 'kitling', and to be weak is described as being 'As weak as a kitling'. Something unpredictable is 'kittle', a mole is a 'mowdie', a wood pigeon a 'cushat', and an owl is a 'howlett'. The spelling of these unusual words varies considerably, and without using phonetic spelling, which is as tedious for the reader and the writer alike, the best way to attain proficiency in the Northumbrian speech is to frequent the many marts and sales which take place, the local point-to-point meetings and the many agricultural shows, especially those such as the shepherds', which are held in the upper reaches of the river valleys.

Dialect is a heritage, it breathes history and tradition, and must never be confused with slang and colloquialisms.

Long may Northumbrians 'Set their friends home after they've had them for their suppers'.

3

Four Famous Northumbrians

Let us now praise famous men.
—Ecclesiasticus

THERE have been many famous Northumbrians, differing in character and in their contributions to the history of their country and county as much as the Northumbrian saints from the Border raiders. This chapter gives brief sketches of the lives of four of the county's famous sons; these men, whose names are still remembered, form a cross section of Society. All had different backgrounds, and each one in his particular way reached the top of his trade or profession.

Roger Thornton, Newcastle's own Dick Whittington, was a poor boy who became the richest merchant in Newcastle in the fourteenth and fifteenth centuries, and was eight times elected Mayor. John Scott, the son of a coal-fitter, became Lord Chancellor of England and was raised to the peerage as Lord Eldon. Charles, Earl Grey, of the ancient family of that name, became Prime Minister and will be remembered for all time as 'Grey of the Reform Bill'. And John Graham Lough was a sculptor, with little or no education, born on the Northumberland—Durham border at Black Hedley.

Certainly the most romantic story is that of Roger Thornton; it is so much so that it reads more like fiction than fact. It is not even known where he came from, although there are many suppositions, one of which is that the future first Mayor of Newcastle came from the little Northumbrian village of Netherwitton, then known as Witton. Certainly some of his descendants lived there until the end of the eighteenth century when the male line died out. A couplet of which there are many different versions runs:

> At the West Gate cam' Thornton in,
> With hap, a ha'penny, and a lamb's skin.

Hap in the sense used here means good luck. Heslop, in his *Northumberland Words*, quotes this couplet, and says it is an ancient Scottish proverb. Roger Thornton, wherever he came from, certainly had more than his share of luck.

Thornton's early life is obscure, and it was not until 1394 that his name appeared in local records as part owner of a ship *The Good Year*. He must have had the Midas touch as everything with which he was connected turned to gold. When Henry IV ascended the throne, Roger Thornton was chosen by his fellow burgesses to represent them in Parliament. The City of Newcastle was separated from the County of Northumberland in 1400, when the King granted a charter to that effect and in the words of those times the City was "to be called the County of the Town of Newcastle for ever". Newcastle could now elect a Sheriff of its own, and the wealthy merchant, who had been a poor boy, became the first Mayor, under the new régime, an office he was to occupy eight times, which must surely be a record.

Newcastle is indebted to this generous merchant prince for the Guildhall, which he built for the use of the Merchant Venturers and the various guilds. He also built a hospital on the Sandhill, known as The Maison Dieu or Thornton's Hospital. He was described by Leland the historian as "wonderful rich" and "the richest merchant that was ever living in Newcastle".

Not only did this enterprising man lease lead mines in Weardale from the Bishop of Durham, but he was also a ship-owner, and dealt in corn and imported wine. Leland, who seems to have been extremely interested in Roger Thornton's business activities, suggests that silver ore was seized from the ships of the King's enemies! Perhaps a little piracy was also part of this man of many enterprises.

Thornton seems to have been on very good terms with the King, and was handsomely compensated for losses he incurred during the rebellion led by the Earl of Northumberland. Investing in property like so many rich men, he acquired in Northumberland, Windgates (Wingates?) Witton (Netherwitton), Stanton, Horsley, Stannington, Benton, Killingworth and Plessey, 'besides houses and tenements in London and Newcastle'. He was in fact the Tyneside tycoon of the Middle Ages. He enjoyed a prosperity not seen again on Tyneside until the Industrial Revolution, when the expansion of the coal-trade and the founding of the many shipyards enriched several local families. With the value of money in Roger Thornton's day it is doubtful if any were ever as "wonderful rich" as the man with the mysterious background who undoubtedly had more than his share of 'hap'.

Unfortunately very little is known of Thornton's private life. He married an Agnes Waunton or Wauton of whom, apart from the fact that she died in 1411 and had several children, nothing at all is known. Their home was in Broad Chare, the word 'chare' meaning a narrow lane. In 1800 there were as many as twenty-one chares on the Quayside alone, including Broad Chare, so named because it was wide enough for horses and carts to be driven along. Many of these chares were destroyed by the fire of 1854: now old Newcastle is being destroyed by the planners in the name of progress.

It was in his house in Broad Chare that Roger Thornton died in 1439 or 1440, and was buried beside his wife in All Saints' Church, where a handsome tomb was erected, only the brass of which remains. Only one of the many children survived his father to inherit the vast fortune, which according to the seven-page Will of "the richest merchant that ever was dwelling in Newcastle" was left entirely to this son. He was also a Roger and had a distinguished career. He was High Sheriff of Northumberland in 1457, a member of the Skinners' Company, and a Commissioner for Truces with Scotland in 1465 and 1466. Sometime before 1428 he made an advantageous marriage with a daughter of Lord Dacre who had estates in Cumberland. There were two daughters of this marriage, one of them married a Lumley, a member of one of the oldest families in the County of Durham.

The Thorntons are outstanding examples of a success story,

and it seems strange that so much is known about their public lives and so little of their origins. By his gifts to the city and the stained glass window in the east end of the Cathedral Church of St Nicholas, which was given by Roger Thornton the elder in his lifetime, he made quite sure that he would be remembered by future generations.

Newcastle also remembers Roger Thornton by a small statue which is in a niche on the frontage of Boots the Chemists in Northumberland Street. Three other Northumbrians who also have statues in this rather incongruous situation are Harry Hotspur, the Champion of the County, Thomas Bewick and Sir John Marley who defended the City against the Scots in 1644, described as the defender of Newcastle:

> Oh, what a brave knight was Governor Marley!
> Stout Sir John Marley!
> Who fought late and early;
> Though the garrison liv'd, and fed rather bar'ley.

Two of the Royal Grammar School's most distinguished old boys are John Scott, later lord Eldon, who became Lord Chancellor and his equally distinguished brother William, who became Lord Stowell. They are both mentioned in the School song:

> Many a name on the scroll of fame
>   Is the heritage of our land;
> Collingwood, Armstrong, Eldon and Bourne,
>   Akenside, Stowell and Brand.
> Strong in their wisdom, wise in their strength,
>   Wielders of sword and pen,
> Far went they forth from the School of the North,
>   That mother and maker of men.
> *"Fortiter defendit triumphans"*.

Eldon Square, Eldon Place and Stowell Street also commemorate the Scott brothers. Eldon Square is under a 'development' threat, while the Georgian houses have disappeared from Eldon Place which is now the property of the ever expanding University of Newcastle.

The eighteenth century is notable for the many outstanding

men which Northumberland produced, and none more so than John Scott, who by his elopement with Bessie Surtees has an aura of romance. The Scott brothers' ancestry is only traceable to their grandfather, William, who was a clerk in the office of a hostman or coal-fitter on the Quayside, while their father, also a William, was apprenticed to a hostman. There is an erroneous impression that Eldon and Stowell, as they became, were sons of poor parents, which was not the case at all. When William Scott died he was able to leave his family property valued at between £30,000 and £40,000. Setting up on his own, the father of the future Lord Chancellor and a Judge of the High Court of Admiralty, became a coal-fitter for the Bowes family, who were colliery owners in the County of Durham, and until the nationalization of the mines traded as John Bowes and Partners. By a marriage with a Lyon of Glamis, the name was hyphenated to Bowes-Lyon, hence the connection of the Queen Mother with the north of England.

William Scott was not only a coal-fitter; he also owned a public house on the Quayside for the many keelmen then employed on the Tyne, as well as many other business interests principally connected with mining. He married twice, and his second wife, the mother of Eldon and Stowell presented her husband with thirteen children, which included twins on three occasions, so it was necessary for William to make as much money as possible to provide for his large family.

John Scott was born on June 4th 1751, on the anniversary of the birth of George III. The house where he was born was in the delightfully named Love Lane, within the city walls. The boys were given the best education possible at what was then known as the Royal Free Grammar School, both John and William going on to University College Oxford. The coal-fitter was an ambitious man, and his children certainly rewarded him by their future successes.

It was while staying in the County of Durham, at the little town of Sedgefield that the future Lord Eldon saw Bessie Surtees for the first time, and the romance began. Bessie's father was a banker in Newcastle and did not consider young Scott a suitable match for his daughter, and as was usual in those days, the young lady was sent to stay with relations as far away from the North as possible, and to all intents and purposes the romance was at an end. In due course Bessie came home to the house on the Quayside which was then called Milbanke House, having been at one time the town house of the Milbanke family (Anne Isabella Milbanke became the wife of Lord Byron the poet—Bessie Surtees and her John had much happier lives than the unfortunate Lady Byron).

It was on the night of the eighteenth of November 1772 that the future Lady Eldon climbed from a window of the house which now bears her name, and she and John fled by post-chaise to Scotland where they were married. In the course of time Aubone Surtees forgave his daughter and accepted his son-in-law, when a second marriage ceremony was conducted according to English law. For a time John Scott contemplated taking Holy Orders but abandoned this idea and instead read for the Bar, to which he was called in 1776. He gives a description of their financial situation in his own words: "Bessie and I thought all our troubles were over; business was to pour in, and we were to be almost rich immediately. So I made a bargain with her, that during the following year all the money I should receive in the first eleven months should be mine, and whatever I got in the twelfth month should be hers. What a stingy dog I must have been to make such a bargain; I would not have done so afterwards. But, however, so it was; that this was our agreement; and how do you think it turned out? In the twelfth month I received half a guinea; eighteen pence went for fees, and Bessie got nine shillings; in the other eleven months I got one shilling." So began the career of the man who was one day to sit on the Woolsack! It was not long before the outstanding abilities of this young northern advocate were realised and his practice at the Bar became considerable.

In 1783 John Scott entered Parliament as a member for a pocket borough in Dorset, and in 1799 he was created a peer, taking the title of Baron Eldon of Eldon, the name of an estate near Bishop Auckland in the Bishopric of Durham, which he had bought in 1792. The manor and the land, of which there were 1,540 acres, cost £22,000. In 1801 the son of the coal-fitter became Lord Chancellor of England, which office he held, with only one break for nearly twenty-five years. An ardent admirer of 'Young Billie Pitt' as Charles James Fox nicknamed the youngest Prime Minister in all English history and a favourite of the Prince Regent, Lord Eldon was created an earl when 'Prinny' ascended the throne.

Bessie his devoted wife, who had risked her family's wrath for love of the young John Scott of long ago, predeceased her famous husband by seven years. She is buried far away from Northumberland, in the Dorset village of Kingston, where the Lord Chancellor on his death at the age of eighty-six was laid beside her.

Lord and Lady Eldon left four children among whom a fortune of nearly three-quarters of a million was divided—a far cry from their first years of marriage when John Scott was a struggling young barrister. Lord Eldon and his brother Lord Stowell brought fame to their native city and to their old school, and both are worthy of their place, not only in the history of Newcastle and Northumberland but in the history of England.

The background of Charles Grey, who became Prime Minister is a complete contrast to that of his fellow Northumbrian Lord Eldon. Lord Grey would be described today as belonging to the Establishment, with all the privileges of the landed gentry. The Greys are first mentioned in Northumbrian history in the reign of Edward I, and held lands at Heaton, Wark, Chillingham, Howick and Bitchfield. Later Fallodon passed by marriage into the possession of this ancient family, and for all time Fallodon will be not only remembered as the birthplace of a Prime Minister, but as the home of another Grey, Sir Edward, who was Foreign Secretary when the First World War was declared. Politics seem to have been in the Greys' blood, although in the early years and in the Middle Ages they were occupied with fighting and intrigue. One member of the family rightly or wrongly was accused of treason, which Shakespeare would have us believe was inspired by the promise of French gold. In *Henry V* the plot is discovered at Southampton before the King sets sail for France:

... one Richard Earl of Cambridge, and the second,
Henry, Lord Scroop of Masham, and the third,
Sir Thomas Grey, knight of Northumberland,
Have for the guilt of France—O guilt indeed—
Confirm'd conspiracy with fearful France,
And by their hands this grace of kings must die—
If Hell and treason hold their promises—
Ere he takes ship for France, and in Southampton.

Shakespeare's history is not always accurate, and the Holinshed
Chronicles, which the greatest dramatist used so freely give a
different version of the substance of the famous traitor's speech.
It is historical fact that Sir Thomas Grey was executed and his
head was sent to Newcastle to be placed on one of the gates, as
was the barbarous custom of those troubled times. Through the
centuries the Greys were often in the thick of events, some serving their country as Sheriffs, and others as Members of Parliament.
At last peace came to Northumberland and like many other great
families the Greys began to interest themselves in their vast
estates. In 1806 the earldom was created. It was Charles the father
of the great reformer who became the first Earl Grey.

The first Earl had married a kinswoman, whose name was also
Grey, and as so many generations of the family have borne the
same christian names, it is confusing to trace the various branches.

Fallodon lies in the north-east corner of Northumberland not
far from the sea. With the coming of the railway in the nineteenth
century, a special stop was made at Fallodon for the convenience
of the Grey family. This ceased only in 1934. The Greys are no
longer at Fallodon, which is now the home of Colonel the
Hon. H. G. O. Bridgeman, D.S.O.

The future Prime Minister was born at Fallodon on March
13th 1764. At the early age of six the child was sent to a preparatory school at Marylebone, and from there his education followed
the conventional pattern of the upper classes, Eton followed by
Cambridge. As was the custom of the times Charles Grey made
the 'Grand Tour', afterwards succeeding Lord Algernon Percy as
a member of Parliament for his native County of Northumberland. Most of his long life (he was 82 when he died at Howick in

The Monument to Grey of the Reform Bill
Bessie Surtees eloped from here

1845) was spent in the world of politics. A Whig and an ardent reformer, both in the Commons and in the House of Lords, he fought for the reformation of the electoral system. Time and again his proposals were defeated by the reactionary members of both the Whig and Tory parties. On the elevation of his father to the peerage, Charles Grey was known by his courtesy title of Lord Howick, and became First Lord of the Admiralty. He sponsored Bills for the abolition of slavery and the emancipation of the Catholics. After a period at the Admiralty he became Foreign Secretary and leader of the House of Commons. These were stormy days in Europe; the horrors of the French Revolution were still fresh in the minds of the people, who were largely against reform, and it was not until the Reform Bill had been defeated on several occasions that Grey's dream at last was realized. In 1832 the Bill was passed.

Summoned by William IV to form a ministry, Earl Grey as he was now, was the first Northumbrian to become Prime Minister of his country. The House was in a state of uproar and Grey's passage was a stormy one. He had fought long and valiantly for the much needed reforms, and his greatest contribution to history, which he first proposed in 1797 was not achieved until he was an old man.

His plan for Parliamentary reform was at last a reality. The number of Members was increased, and householders were each allowed to vote. The days of the 'rotten boroughs' were over and an end was made to bribery and corruption. Earl Grey's life spanned four reigns and was spent in the years which saw radical changes in Britain and Europe.

Grey was born in the reign of George III and the young Victoria had been on the throne for eight years when he died in Northumberland, far away from the struggle and turmoil of Westminster. During those four reigns dramatic events took place, in many of which Grey participated. In his early years in the House he would listen to the verbal battles between Pitt and Fox, who were orators as well as statesmen. He saw the rise and fall of Napoleon. He took part in the celebrations for Nelson's victories, and when the great sailor died at Trafalgar, it was a fellow Northumbrian,

D

Blagdon in Winter
The Hall at Capheaton

Admiral Collingwood, who took over the command. These were years of unrest until at last an uneasy peace followed Wellington's defeat of Napoleon's army at Waterloo, and no doubt Grey took part in the peace celebrations which followed the victory. Tragedies and comedies were played out in the glare of the public as in the case of the pathetic, unbalanced George III. His flamboyant heir the Prince Regent ordered the door of Westminster Abbey to be locked during his coronation to make sure that Queen Caroline was unable to enter. The Royal Divorce followed, which divided the country, and when 'Prinny's' ten years on the throne came to an end he was succeeded by the mediocre William IV with his sobriquet of 'Silly Billie'. In 1837, the young Victoria was crowned, and Melbourne was Prime Minister.

Charles Grey ranks with the greatest of Northumberland's sons. The monument at the top of Grey Street in Newcastle, and the name of the street commemorate his memory in the City and County of Newcastle. In 1794 he had married the daughter of Lord Ponsonby, and they had a large family, many of whom survived their famous father, 'Grey of the Reform Bill'.

The life story of John Graham Lough is a typical example of the poor boy of genius who made good, and is a striking contrast to the lives of Thornton the merchant adventurer, Eldon the Lord Chancellor and Grey the statesman. Lough's birthplace was some miles south of the river Tyne on the southern border of Northumberland, where the land rises steeply to meet the County of Durham. Although many biographies have been written about this boy who became a sculptor of national repute there is disagreement about the actual place of his birth. Some of his biographers maintain that it was at Black Hedley, while others are of the opinion that it was at the nearby hamlet of Greenhead. This Greenhead must not be confused with the village of the same name in South Tynedale.

Lough was born of humble parentage, his father being the village blacksmith. Taking into consideration Lough's background and lack of education his success is all the more amazing. Had he lived in the present days of free education and university grants, he would have received help and encouragement and would not have endured the privations and poverty of his early years. That he did overcome his handicaps makes his success all the more memorable.

One of his biographers says that in his childhood Lough was greatly influenced by the eccentricities of the owner of Black Hedley Hall, whose name was Hopper. This gentleman had a passion for statues and figures of every description with which he ornamented his house, both inside and out. The dovecote was surmounted by figures of shepherds in Highland dress! It is possible that the child was fascinated by these extraordinary ornamentations, but it is doubtful if they inspired his genius. At a very early age the future sculptor began to model 'dollies' with the clay from nearby Greenhead, and he and his brother spent their time making soldiers with which they filled their cottage home.

John Lough's education was negligible. At an early age he was taken from school to work in the fields, and later he was apprenticed to a stonemason, which laid the foundations of his future career. There is one story concerning Lough's youth which is that he made so many 'dollies' that eventually there was no room left for them in the cottage and some of them had to be put in the garden. The Squire of Minsteracres, a house not far away from the boy's home, was a Mr Silvertop, a member of an old Roman Catholic family. The Silvertops only left Minsteracres within the last decade, and the house is now a Passionist monastery. The squire of Lough's day is said to have been coming home from hunting one day and passed the cottage with its statues in the garden. Squire Silvertop, so the story goes, was so much impressed with the boy's work that he befriended him and started him on his future career. It is true that George Silvertop helped the young artist in many ways, but there are so many conflicting versions of this episode in Lough's young life that it is impossible to arrive at the truth. Some writers say that the young apprentice proved himself such an excellent stonemason that he decided to branch out on his own, and that his first commission was a headstone which is in the churchyard at Muggleswick, an isolated

moorland village on the Durham side of the border where the
Loughs were then living.

Another commission for a headstone came from a family
named Stephenson in Allendale in Northumberland. Little would
his patrons think that in the years ahead the humble stonemason
would be commissioned by the great and famous to decorate
their homes and gardens with gigantic statues.

Another version of the Lough story is that after his appren-
ticeship the young man came to work in the City of Newcastle,
and then at the age of 26 decided to try his fortune in faraway
London, making the journey by sailing ship from the Tyne. Yet
another version is that it was Squire Silvertop who encouraged
the boy to leave the North. The Squire's advice was that a study
should be made of sculpture in the British Museum, particularly
of the Elgin Marbles, and that he would pay the expenses of a
visit to Rome where John could study the great masters. It is said
that the young man refused this generous offer, and that his
would-be benefactor was so hurt that he gave up any attempt to
launch the young genius.

The first few years in London are typical of the experiences of
many another artist. Hungry, often without money, Lough
struggled on. The room he worked in was so small that it is said
that he knocked a hole in the ceiling so that his sculptured
figures could stand upright! For this enterprise Lough was
threatened with legal action, but when the lawyer, whom Lough's
landlord consulted, went to see for himself what was going on, he
was so impressed with Lough's work that the action was with-
drawn. It was in 1827 that at last Lough's well deserved success
came. His huge statue of Milo brought him fame. Haydon, the
artist who befriended Lough gives a day to day account of
Lough's success, and it is recorded with all the verbosity of the
nineteenth century.

On June 10th the first exhibition of the sculptor's work was
held in London. This was his 'private view' day, and the great
and famous flocked to his studio. Wellington was there and the
incomparable Mrs Siddons who admired and praised, and from
then onwards, in the language of today, Lough was 'made'.

Elizabeth Barrett Browning mentions him in her poem 'Lady Geraldine's Courtship'.

The live air that waves the lilies waves the slender jet of water,
Like a holy thought sent up from soul of fasting;
Whereby lies a marble silence, sleeping (Lough, the sculptor wrought her)
So asleep she is forgetting to say Hush!—a fancy quaint.

Mark how heavy white her eyelids! not a dream between them lingers;
And the left hand index droppeth from the lips upon the cheek;
While the right hand—with the symbol—rose held slack within the fingers—
Has fallen backward in the basin—yet this Silence will not speak.

John Graham Lough had travelled a long way from his early beginnings in Northumberland. The next forty years were the years of fame and success, and his output was enormous, many of his works being accepted by the Royal Academy. In 1832 he married Mary North, the daughter of the domestic chaplain to the Duke of Kent, Queen Victoria's father. Mary Lough outlived her famous husband by twelve years, and died in London in 1888, leaving two daughters.

After his rise to fame the Loughs travelled widely, spending, as one would expect, a great deal of time in Italy. Lough never forgot his early beginnings, nor the City of Newcastle and the county of his birth where so much of his work can still be seen today. During the time he spent in Newcastle as a young man, he was employed in the building of the Literary and Philosophical Society in Westgate Road. Little would he think that one day his own work would be placed among the works of art in that building. On the staircase today stands his statue of James Losh, who was Recorder of Newcastle and one time President of the Literary and Philosophical Society. Stephenson's Monument in Newcastle and Collingwood's at Tynemouth are both the work of this fellow Northumbrian, while in many of the great houses in the County are other examples of his work.

His creative energy must have been enormous; two of his

largest undertakings are the statues of Queen Victoria which stands outside the Royal Exchange in London and that of the Prince Consort which he was commissioned to execute for Lloyds.

John Graham Lough died in London in 1876. A worthy son of Northumberland, who by sheer hard work achieved fame and his place in the history of his county.

Thornton, Eldon, Grey and Lough rank not only as great Northumbrians but as great Englishmen. They all, without exception, made their contributions to the community and all are examples to future generations that by hard work, determination and ambition of the right kind, circumstances can be overcome and hopes be fulfilled.

4

Blagdon: A Northumbrian Estate

Be of good comfort Master Ridley, and play the man.
We shall this day light such a candle by God's
grace in England, as (I trust) shall never be put out.
—Bishop Hugh Latimer (1485?-1555)

NORTHUMBERLAND has more big estates still intact than any other English county. In spite of crippling death duties and the sweeping changes which have taken place in the last fifty years, Northumbrian landowners have held on tenaciously to their inheritance. This is one of Northumberland's greatest assets. There are few absentee landlords; those whose land has been preserved and saved from the housing estates and planners, maintain that spirit of goodwill and friendship which has existed in the county for generations.

Blagdon, the home of the 4th Viscount Ridley, is an outstanding illustration. Lying ten miles north of the busy industrial city of Newcastle and straddling both sides of the Great North Road, Blagdon is unique insomuch that it is on the fringe of the coalfield, so near to Newcastle, and yet retaining its rural atmosphere. Once behind the gateposts surmounted by the white bulls, emblem of the Ridley family, the visitor enters another world. Forgotten is the traffic of the A1 and the sprawling mass of Newcastle.

Run on up-to-date lines, with a total acreage of 8,000, 2,000 of which are under Lord Ridley's personal supervision, Blagdon has retained its rural charm and an atmosphere all its own. As the drive winds through the parklands and the house comes into view, the picture is one which conveys a feeling of continuity, the past and the present meeting in a setting that is so typically

English, and which has so sadly disappeared from the landscape of so many other counties.

Before the Ridleys came to Blagdon in the eighteenth century, a branch of the Northumbrian family of Fenwick had made their home there, followed by the Whites of Newcastle, who laid the foundations of the present house. A marriage between the Whites and the Ridleys united the two families; a Matthew White was created a baronet in 1756, and it was his sister's son by her marriage to Matthew Ridley who became the second baronet, Sir Matthew White Ridley; since then the heirs to the title have all borne the name Matthew White Ridley.

The name of the architect who built the house for Matthew White Ridley is unknown, and Blagdon has been altered considerably since his time. Bourne, the Newcastle historian (whose name occurs in the school song of Newcastle Royal Grammar School), gives this description of Blagdon in 1736: "Since the present gentleman was the possessor, Blagdon vastly surpasses what it was formerly; and whether we consider the stateliness of the house, the grandeur of the avenue, the beauty of the gardens or the art and ornament of the curious fish ponds, we shall find them exceeded by few in the whole country". Although additions have been made, and some of the house demolished after a fire in 1944, Bourne's description is applicable today, although the late Dowager Lady Ridley, in a short history *Blagdon and the Ridleys* says, "It is not a remarkable house". Perhaps it is not remarkable when compared with Blenheim or Chatsworth, but Blagdon is a home, not a museum, a home where the same family, whose members in their various ways have contributed to the history of the county, has lived since the mid-eighteenth century.

The family of Ridley takes its name from a small hamlet in South Tynedale, their name first appearing in records during the thirteenth century. The chief of this powerful clan lived at Willimoteswick, where the most famous of all the Ridleys, Nicholas the Bishop and Martyr, is reputed to have been born. Bishop or not, the Ridleys were not above doing a bit of shifting, or in other words, stealing other people's stock. Raiding and reiving was a major occupation in those lawless days and the Ridleys were no better and no worse than their fellow Borderers and their hereditary enemies the Scots.

In James Hogg, the Ettrick Shepherd's ballad, 'Lock the Door Lariston', the Ridleys receive a 'mention';

> Bewcastle brandishes high his broad scimitar;
> Ridley is riding his fleet footed grey,
> Hidley and Howard there,
> Wandale and Windermere;
> Lock the door, Lariston; hold them at bay.
> Why dost thou smile noble, Elliot of Lariston?
> Why does the joy-candle gleam in thine eye?
> Thou bold Border ranger,
> Beware of thy danger;
> Thy foes are relentless, determined, and nigh.

Until the seventeenth century, the Ridleys ruled supreme in that most lovely district of Northumberland, the peaceful unspoilt country overlooked by Morley Banks, where the united Allens join the South Tyne, and the road winds its way from Ridley by Beltingham to what remains of the fortified tower of Willimoteswick. By their support of Charles I during the Civil War, the 'Broad Knights' were dispossessed of their lands, and the clan scattered. No more would a Ridley ride out from Hardriding on some nefarious mission. Strangers occupied the old house that stood on the north side of the South Tyne between Haltwhistle and Bardon Mill, from which there is a glorious view of South Tynedale. Some of the Ridleys became respectable farmers; others drifted to the town, the far away city of Newcastle. One of these was an enterprising young man named Nicholas after his famous ancestor.

His story is slightly reminiscent of Dick Whittington, for he was Mayor of Newcastle twice, in 1688 and 1707, the year of the Treaty of Union with Scotland, when peace came to the Borders at last. Nicholas Ridley formed a business association with Matthew White, and the foundations were laid by marriage and the growth of the coal trade of the Ridleys of Blagdon.

As their fortunes increased the Ridleys acquired a house beyond the City Wall, Heaton Hall, which has now been demolished to make way for a housing estate. It was from Heaton Hall that the Ridleys went to Blagdon to become countrymen again, although many of them served the city as mayors and the county as Members of Parliament.

Wyatt, the famous architect, was called in to improve and alter the house at Blagdon, and much of his work is visible today in the South and North Lodges, the stables, and the Wyatt Room as it is known, which has been restored to its original colours of 1789. From the east side of the house 'rides' radiate into the woodlands while the south front overlooks the garden and canal designed by Sir Edwin Lutyens, the father of the late Dowager Lady Ridley. This formal garden, with its canal centrepiece, is reminiscent of a French château.

The fourth baronet was a great admirer of the Newcastle sculptor, John Lough, and one of the many examples of his work which are to be seen in the grounds is a statue of Milo in the water garden. So much did the fourth Sir Matthew admire Lough that he declared Michelangelo's work to be inferior: that is very much a matter of opinion.

The gardens of Blagdon alternate between the formal and the near wild. Little wooded denes lead down to a stream, or in the language of Northumberland, a burn, a tributary of the Blyth, a river spanned by a bridge on the Great North Road. The Blyth flows through Plessey Woods on its way to the port of the same name, in which the family have held many interests.

Blagdon is not one of the houses which are regularly open to the public, but in 1965 the Hexham Conservative Association, at the invitation of Viscount and Viscountess Ridley, held a midsummer picnic in the grounds, and the visitors were allowed to see the interior of the historic house and its many treasures. Thousands of people wandered through the grounds, no doubt many of them somewhat astonished to see so much of John Lough's works of art, and within the house itself countless figures of the recumbent Ridley Bulls.

The charm of Blagdon is that it is not a 'half-crown house', relying on the public to maintain it as a home. Though such houses may give pleasure to thousands, they tend to have the atmosphere of museums. Gracious living, so rapidly dying out, is still here at Blagdon.

On the walls hang many family portraits. In 1966, Lord Ridley was successful in regaining for the family the portrait of a bygone Lady Ridley of Blagdon, which had passed out of their possession. In the dining-room is John Snow's picture of 'The Meet at Blagdon', in 1836. The hounds at the time were the private pack of Sir Matthew White Ridley. This picture, with Blagdon in the background is one of the present Lord Ridley's favourites. As is to be expected, there is a portrait of the Marian Martyr, which hangs at the top of the staircase, restored by the third Viscount after the disastrous fire of 1944, when the house was a wartime babies' hospital.

In 1900, the fifth baronet, who had been a member of Lord Salisbury's Cabinet, was offered a peerage, which he accepted, and so became the first Viscount of Blagdon and Blyth.

The record of the Blagdon Ridleys is one of public service; as industrialists and landowners, they were solid and respectable, with one or two exceptions, who, nevertheless add a dash of colour to the family story. The second baronet, whose portrait was painted by Hoppner, obviously had a roving eye, and though a member of Parliament for Morpeth and Mayor of Newcastle, had to pay £400 in damages to a Morpeth doctor. This member of the family, although running true to type as far as his public life was concerned was not only indiscreet but foolish in his private life, as he was caught on the stairs of a house in Newcastle with the doctor's wife in the most compromising circumstances! Neither the baronet's constituents nor the people of Newcastle appeared unduly shocked by this lapse from the straight and narrow path, and for many years he remained in public office. Even his wife seems to have been unperturbed by his extra marital relations. Perhaps the raiding blood was still running strong through the veins of the Ridleys; cattle and sheep were not the only prizes lifted.

The brides who have come to Blagdon throughout the years have left shadows of their personalities behind. Each one had her different ideas about 'improvements', some are remembered for their virtues, and others for the sometimes not favourable impression they made upon their tenants, servants and neighbours. There was the 'Proud Lady', with her delusions of grandeur, who could never settle down, but moved from house to house in an unsuccessful attempt to find peace and happiness. She was the wife of the third baronet, and bore him twelve children in the course of sixteen years. Ten of the children survived, a record in those days, when a high rate of infant mortality was taken as a matter of course. In some ways, this extraordinary woman was ahead of her times, and she had all her children inoculated against smallpox. The *Newcastle Courant* of 1791 reported that "Lady Ridley had given direction that all the poor children in the parish of Stannington, whose parents were willing, should be innoculated at her expense, and that upwards of sixty had received the benefit of Her Ladyship's benevolance and recovered".

Apart from this enterprise the 'Proud Lady', Laura Hawkins, as she was born, treated her family in the most heartless and extraordinary manner, and finally became estranged from all but her son Matthew. How incongruous that it should be she who became mother-in-law of the most charming and pathetic of all the brides, Cecilia, whose presence (she could never haunt) still remains in the house where for a few short years she was a wife and mother.

In 1958, the late Lady Ridley, wife of the third Viscount, edited a collection of Cecilia's letters.[1] It is one of the most delightful collections of letters ever written, and obviously edited with loving care. Writers and historians owe a debt of gratitude to Lady Ridley for preserving these intimate and very human accounts of the life and times of such an interesting young woman as Cecilia Ridley must have been.

Cecilia was the daughter of James Parke, the son of a Liverpool merchant, who had a brilliant career, was called to the Bar, and was created a peer, taking the title of Wensleydale. None of his sons survived him; the title became extinct, but was revived by his grandson, the first Viscount Ridley, who took it as his second title.

[1] Published by Rupert Hart-Davis.

Cecilia Parke was born in 1819, and had the happiest of child-hoods. Her education was the conventional one of that time for a young lady of her social standing; lessons from governesses, a knowledge of foreign languages, painting in water colours, and visits when in London to various places of interest. Lady Ridley says that from the age of fifteen Cecilia kept a journal, but al-though informative, it is not nearly so interesting nor so amusing as her letters.

In 1837, when Queen Victoria ascended the throne, Cecilia 'came out'. She gives vivid descriptions of the parties and balls she attended, with many outspoken comments on the looks and behaviour of London society. Naturally, anyone so attractive as Cecilia had many admirers, whom she described in letters to an aunt. After the London season, the Parke family rented a house from the Duke of Bedford, Ampthill Park, which is now a Cheshire Home.

Unfortunately, Cecilia does not reveal how she met the man whom the Victorians would have described as 'her fate', the Northumbrian Matthew White Ridley of Blagdon. Twelve years older than his bride, this Baronet was more of a countryman than his immediate ancestors, and took a practical interest in his vast estates. A serious minded young man, he was also a keen sports-man, who hunted three days a week, and was an able shot. Matthew Ridley was considered by Cecilia's mother to be a most suitable husband for her dearly loved daughter, even though the distance between the two families would lead to long separations. In 1841, Matthew married his Cecilia, and took her to Shoreham for their honeymoon, from which place Cecilia wrote to her mother, giving numerous details of the house in which the honey-moon was spent, the books which the newly married couple read, and her obvious happiness with her husband to whom she refers formally as 'Sir M'.

It was in October that Cecilia came to Blagdon, after what must have been a most uncomfortable journey of three days. Northumberland is an unknown county today, and in 1841 it must have appeared to the young bride that she had come to a foreign land. Yet in the four short years which Cecilia had to live, she learned to love the mellow stone house, which today looks very much the same as she saw it. In her many letters to her mother she describes the duties she performed, her interviews with the housekeeper, the gardens, and the surrounding countryside. Stannington, the nearest village to Blagdon, which is divided by the Great North Road, did not in those days make a favourable impression on the girl from the South. She thought the cottages small and mean; how delighted she would be to see the Stannington of today with its modernized cottages and well kept gardens.

Descendants of the many people Cecilia met (and sometimes criticized) are still living in Northumberland. Alnwick is still the home of the Dukes of Northumberland, and although Ravensworth Castle in County Durham, which Cecilia visited, has been demolished, Lord Ravensworth, head of the Liddell family has estates in Northumberland at Eslington.

The Old or Georgian Assembly Rooms in Newcastle, where Sir Matthew took his young wife to receptions and balls, is no longer the scene of the most important Newcastle functions, and its future existence is in the balance. In 1967 Her Royal Highness Princess Margaret was entertained at Blagdon before attending a dance in the same rooms where Cecilia had danced and observed with such devastating accuracy the character and behaviour of other guests. Gentle and sweet as she was, some of the derogatory remarks she made in her letters regarding some of the county families must have caused their descendants to smile.

In July 1842, Cecilia became a mother. Her son was born in London presumably so that she could be near her parents. 'Little Matt', as the baby was known, was christened in the house at Blagdon "because of the cold damp weather". These cold northern winters must have affected Cecilia's delicate constitution and accelerated the seeds of the tuberculosis which in those days was accepted with apparent fatalism.

It was at Blagdon that Matthew and Cecilia's second son was born, only a few days after her beloved sister Mary had given birth, also to a son. Mary, who had married a Howard, died a few days afterwards, and this was the greatest grief of Cecilia's short life. In July of 1844 Cecilia gave birth to twins. The boy survived for only three weeks, Mary the daughter growing up in a mother-less home.

After the births Cecilia's health deteriorated rapidly. Little seems to have been done to arrest the disease from which this young wife and mother was to die so tragically in 1845, leaving behind her three small children and a husband, who, although he loved her dearly and never married again, had no compunction in impressing upon Cecilia the fact that she was dying!

So ended the short reign of Cecilia at Blagdon, but she has left so many memories behind her, that even today, more than a century after her death, her personality is so strong, that one cannot think of Blagdon without thinking of Cecilia. How happy she would be could she see the house now, a home where children's laughter can be heard, where another 'Little Matt' plays in the gardens, and where lives another Cecilia, one of her great-great-granddaughters.

The house has had many distinguished visitors in its history; among them the Prince of Wales, later Edward VII, for whom the first bathroom was installed! When the then Mr Churchill came to Newcastle in 1950, he was entertained by the third Viscount Ridley.

The third Viscount was one of Northumberland's most distinguished sons. For a time he was Deputy Lord Lieutenant of the County, and Chairman of the Council of King's College, then part of the University of Durham, and now a university in its own right. He was twice elected chairman of the Northumberland County Council, the first time at the early age of 37, and has now been succeeded by his son, the fourth Viscount—the third generation of the family to hold this position. Intensely interested in all things mechanical, the third Viscount was also chairman of Consett Iron Company and an Honorary Colonel of the Northumberland Hussars. The present Viscount is also active in the public affairs of his county. His mother the late Dowager was extremely interested in child welfare and when Blagdon was a Babies' Hospital during the last war she acted as theatre sister.

The present Lord Ridley married a daughter of the Earl of Scarbrough, Lady Anne Lumley, in 1953. The wedding took place in Durham Cathedral, as the Lumleys are one of the oldest families in that county. A story has been handed down through the generations that when James VI of Scotland succeeded to the throne of England to become James I, he was entertained by the Lumleys within the Bishopric of Durham. The Lumleys of that day were very anxious to impress their new sovereign with their ancient lineage, so much so that the King became tired of their efforts, and in 'braid Scots' exclaimed that he "Never kenned afore that Adam was a Lumley"!

Few families can hold a higher record of public service to their county than do the Ridleys of Blagdon; their name is interwoven in the history of Northumberland. Secure in their historic home, so secluded yet so alive, surrounded by the land they have cared for so well, the Blagdon Ridleys have vindicated the words of the verse:

> So fell the Ridley's ancient line,
> Lord William's ancient towers,
> Fair Ridley by the silver Tyne,
> And sweet Thorngrafton's Bowers.

Eclipsed for a time after the Civil Wars, the Ridleys have regained their rightful place in Northumberland's story.

The writer, who is proud to bear the name of Ridley, is sure that in the years ahead, when histories of Northumberland are written, surely Blagdon will receive the attention it deserves, and an account of the part its owners have played in the pattern of Northumbrian life. Long may the famous white bulls remain a landmark on the Great North Road.

Cecilia Ridley, from the painting by F. Stone

5

Border Legends

Over the Borderland, wha' will gan' wi' me,
Buckle your horses and sharpen your blades,
We will bring back with us good Scottish cattle,
Good Scottish horses and fair Scottish maids.
—C. F. Palmer

THE original definition of a legend was a chronicle or register of the lives of saints formerly read at matins or refections. As these included any marvellous story or incident respecting the saints, legends came to mean any ancient tale whether authentic or not. A more modern definition is a story based on historical fact, embroidered and embellished and handed down from one generation to another. Today many of these legends appear ridiculous and impossible, but are based on fact that has gathered momentum in the telling.

Very few people are guiltless of the temptation to add a little when it comes to repeating a good story to make it even better. In the past when so many people, especially in an isolated county such as Northumberland, were illiterate, the stories were repeated by word of mouth and lost nothing in the telling. All through history legends have sprung up of the exploits of the famous and of the many battles which have been fought on Northumbrian soil. Superstition, so rife in the past, regarded what are normal events today as works of the devil and the supernatural.

The legends connected with St Cuthbert, Northumbria's most famous saint, which will forever be associated with that little group of islands, the Farnes, lying off the incomparable coast of Northumberland, are countless and have been recounted many

E

The chapel on Inner Farne

times. St Cuthbert was a shepherd boy who dedicated his life to God and was consecrated at York seventh Bishop of Lindisfarne. He loved the birds (which even today find sanctuary on the Farnes) and as with St Francis of Assisi it is said that they fed from his hands. The eider ducks for many years have been known as St Cuthbert's chicks, and some small pebbles, still found on the shores of the islands, as St Cuthbert's beads. 'Cuddy's' Caves in Northumberland are named after St Cuthbert; there is one not far inland at Howburn near the hamlet of Lowick, and another near Doddington in Glendale. The Saint travelled after his death more than he ever did in life—the reputed resting places of his bones are numerous in the northern counties. It was on the advice of a wise woman near Chester-le-Street, in the Bishopric of Durham, that the monks followed the 'dun cow' to Dunholm the old name for what is now a city and county, and at last the wanderings came to an end where Durham's Norman Cathedral stands today. The bones of St Cuthbert found peace at last.

One of the lesser known legends surrounding the monks and their journeys with their precious burden of saintly bones, is connected with the North Tyne family of Dodd and appears in a small booklet written by Edward Charlton, M.D. in 1870 and is as follows: "... of the fourth name that of Dodds, distinct records even of the name are given us by the right early writer Reginald of Durham, who flourished about the year 1150. Hence we have almost the first historic trace of North Tynedale story.

"Reginald tells us that when the Danes first burst upon Lindisfarne, in the seventh century, the monks bore off into the mountains the body of St Cuthbert. From place to place they transported it, till their number, by famine and desolation, was reduced to four. And one of these was Eilaf; and he and his companions were exhausted by hunger, and they had no food save the salted head of a horse and a single cheese. And Eilaf longed for this cheese, till so great was his desire thereof that he hid it and began to eat it. And at noon the bearers of St Cuthbert's body rested in a desert place, and sought to make their mid-day meal; and behold, the cheese on which they had relied was missing.

"Then the brethren prayed that the thief might be changed into a fox, and so there issued straightway from a wood a fox, with the identical cheese in its jaws, which the animal vainly tried to devour, and as vainly to get rid of, and much laughter did this cause unto the brethren; and they knew that he now writhed before them in the shape of a fox.

"And they having been sufficiently amused, did pray to God, and St Cuthbert, to restore to him his human shape: and from that day, all the race of Eilaf did bear the name of Dodd, which, in the mother tongue signifies a fox."

This legend is one of the most curious concerning surnames, as these descendants of a monk became some of the most notorious of the Border raiders and were one of the famous 'graynes' or clans of the wild but beautiful valley of the North Tyne.

There are many legends all over the country with this recurring theme of a human being transformed into an animal; the famous Laidley (loathsome) Worm of Spindlestone Heugh is typical, and has been described in the writer's previous book *Portrait of Northumberland*.

The Northumbrian Legend with the greatest number of variations is the 'Long Pack' which like the fox legend also has background of North Tynedale. Practically every castle and Pele tower, every river and little burn have their local folk tales, and it is often in long forgotten village histories that these are discovered. Buried treasure is hidden all over the county, from the river Allen below Staward Pele to the little sheets of water that lie north of Hadrian's Wall.

Water seems to have an attraction for the minstrel and ballad monger, though few have been so ambitious as the people of Morpeth who attempted to make their river, the Wansbeck, tidal! A glance at the map will show that the Morpethians were somewhat optimistic. No doubt they thought that if Morpeth could become an inland port it would rival Newcastle on the then thriving river Tyne, where the ships loaded and unloaded on the Quayside. The story is that there was living at that time, (no specific date is given), a wizard named Michael Scott who had given miraculous help to a King of France. Consequently this worker of spells was summoned to Morpeth, where he directed the inhabitants how to carry out their plan. The most general version is that a young man was to run from the mouth of the river to Morpeth, a distance of several miles, without looking back, and the tide would follow him. Pursued by the incoming tide the young man ran as far as Sheepwash, where the roar of the water was such that he broke the spell by looking back. The tide immediately receded to join the North Sea at what was then called Camboise Bay.

W. W. Tomlinson, in his invaluable *Guide to Northumberland*, says that the strangely named Sheepwash is a corruption of 'Ship-wash', as at one time small vessels sailed upstream as far as the wash, or ford.

In the wild country of the Wannys where the Wansbeck rises a local poet and writer, James Armstrong was inspired to sing the praises of the river that Michael Scott could not control. In a verse of his poem 'Wild Hills O' Wannys', he wrote,

> There's the Reed an' the Wansbeck, where the dews sweetly fa',
> The Lyles Burn and Reasey we oft fisht them a',
> Aye, there's monie a burnie and sweet heather brae
> Round the wild hills o' Wannys sae far, far away.

This James Armstrong apparently lived at the village of Ridsdale which is one of the most confusing place names in Northumberland. Where Watling Street makes a sharp descent from the south towards the river Reed, there is the wild valley which is sometimes referred to as Ridsdale, sometimes as Redesdale and yet again as the Rede Water! The village of Ridsdale sprang up in the last century when, for about fifteen years, iron works were developed there by the then Sir William G. Armstrong. This is some of the wildest and most barren country in all Northumberland.

James Armstrong published his book in its second edition in 1879, and it is described as "*Wanny Blossoms*. A book of Song, with a brief treatise on Fishing, with the fly, worm, minnow and roe; Sketches from Border Life, and Fox and Otter Hunting. Price 2/6 in extra cloth binding, by post for 33 stamps. To be had from the author, or from The Hexham Herald, Hexham." Opinion may vary as to Armstrong's poetical gifts, yet they have a certain charm, and convey his great love of his county, especially Redesdale, and the surrounding country.

In a poem dedicated to 'Our Border Chief', W. H. Charlton of Hesleyside near Bellingham expresses nostalgia for the days of Border raiding, though had he lived in those far off days he may not have waxed so poetical over the exploits of Scots and Northumbrians who have written their names in the annals of Border warfare. The two following verses are from the ballad 'Our Glorious Borderland'.

> Nae mair adown yon lonely dells
> Will dauntless Bowrie ride,
> Or 'Kinmont Wullie', or 'Gilknockie',
> Nor brave 'Jock o' the Syde',
> By Border Peel, in glittering steel,
> Wi' a true and gallant band—
> My heart yet swells o' them to tell,
> In our glorious Borderland.
> An' yonder's Darden's dusky peak,
> And Wanny's sunny brow,
> Beside where sparkling crystal streams
> An' mountain burnies flow;
> An' Cheviot's wild and shaggy crest,
> High o'er them a' sae grand,
> O'er 'Chevy Chase' and 'Otterburn',
> In our Glorious Borderland.

Many are the legends that have grown up through the centuries of the deeds of the raiders, and Redesdale was the heart of the raiding country, sharing with North Tynedale the reputation of being a land of outlaws and thieves. The writer of *Wanny Blossoms* may have romanticized the deeds of such wild men as Bowrie, who belonged to the Charlton Clan, and Kinmont Wullie, a Scottish Armstrong who made a dramatic escape from Carlisle Castle; but it is in his articles on fishing and hunting, nearly a hundred years ago, that this ardent admirer of his county comes into his own. It is interesting too, that in these accounts of long-ago hunts and fishing in the Border streams, that the same names appear that are mentioned in current hunting reports; many descendants of the Border raiders still go out with the Border Hunt. Kinmont Wullie's memory was revived when in 1961 a horse bearing his name won the Scottish Grand National.

A great deal of smuggling took place in these Border valleys and there is a legend that Brandy Bank, which is the steep descent into West Woodburn from the south, is so named from an incident when an illicit cask of brandy was overturned on the steep bank, or brae as Northumberland describes a hill.

From Woodburn the road rises steeply on its way north to join the road to Carter Bar. At Elishaw the road from Newcastle to Jedburgh is joined by Watling Street. This is a land of battles and feuds, some long since forgotten, while others such as Otterburn are immortalized in verse. 'The Raid of the Redesweir' and 'The Death of Parcy Reed' have been told in verse throughout the centuries. This is the country of illicit liquor stills; and of lonely tracks through the Cheviots which the smugglers used. The cattle are now driven over the Border to be sold at the Northumbrian Marts, and not 'lifted' as they were in days gone by.

In 1916 John and Jean Lang wrote in collaboration their *Stories of the Border Marches* and so helped to preserve many legends. There is no doubt that many records have been destroyed as of no value, which would have been treasured today by those who wish to preserve for future generations the tales of their forebears. The Northumberland Women's Institutes, in common with other counties in England and Wales, compiled Village Scrap Books in their Golden Jubilee Year, and by doing so have rendered a service to the historians of the future.

Close to Watling Street at Fourlaws farm there is a Roman milestone, which tradition says was the stone the ill-fated Earl of Derwentwater used as a mounting block when he and his little band of followers gathered in this lonely country and made their fatal decision to raise the Stuart standard in the 'Fifteen'.

That this is a Roman milestone, there is no doubt though it is not at the roadside; a study of the map shows that the present Watling Street has in one or two places deviated from the road of the Romans; but that it is Derwentwater's stone is open to question, as the most reliable evidence is that the Jacobites gathered at Greenrigg, which is on the east side of Watling Street, close to the romantically named Waterfalls. There was an encampment at Fourlaws, used as a signal station by the Romans to warn those garrisons on the military road at Limestone Bank, west of Chollerford, of approaching danger.

The tragic figure of James Radcliffe, third Earl of Derwentwater will never be forgotten in Northumberland, and many are the stories which have grown round this young man, who was the victim of his Stuart blood. In Surtees' Ballad 'Farewell to pleasant Dilston Hall' a verse mentions the bonny gray steed, which is connected with the controversial mounting block;

> And fare thee well, my bonny gray steed,
> That carried me aye so free;
> I wish I had been asleep in my bed
> The last time I mounted thee;
> The warning bell now bids me cease
> My trouble's nearly o'er;
> Yon sun that rises from the sea
> Shall rise on me no more.

In Derwentwater's own country near Dilston on the Devilswater, there is a superstition that no one can cross the burn should they be carrying a pack of playing cards, but that if, when crossing the bridge between Corbridge and Hexham (it spans the Devilswater as it runs to meet the Tyne), both feet are raised from the ground at the same time, any wish will be granted. How this feat is accomplished has not been explained!

Far from Derwentwater country in the Cheviot Hills (which form not only a barrier between Northumberland and Scotland, but a deep penetration into England), is the awe inspiring chasm of Henhole. Lying a little to the south-west of the Muckle Cheviot is this freak of nature. Even on a summer's day Henhole is sinister, and its legend even more so; local people believed it was haunted by fairies.

Long before there was a College Valley pack of foxhounds, the fox was hunted in this land of sheep. Some say there was a pack at Kirknewton, a village which nestles under the shadow of Yeavering Bell, that was trencher fed (i.e. boarded out). Riding the hardy little hill ponies, the shepherds, who regarded the fox as their greatest enemy, had a poor opinion of one of their followers, an old man who could only afford an aged mare. Had they but realised, it was to be the slowness of the despised mare which saved the old man's life. One winter's day a fox was raised near Kirknewton, which led the hunt into the heart of the Cheviot country, towards the dreaded Henhole. Far behind the hunt came the old man on his mare, which by this time was so tired that the rider dismounted and led it by the bridle. The pack was now in full cry and pursued their quarry to the edge of the ravine, where all disappeared into its depths. The less intrepid of the riders, when they reached the haunted ravine, were all for calling off hounds, but the more reckless decided to carry on. Suddenly ghostly music was heard, and the terrified horses plunged their riders into Henhole and certain death. It was long afterwards that the old man and his mare came on the scene, and seeing the cliff edge ploughed up by the horses' hoofs, and knowing the dark reputation of Henhole and its ghostly inhabitants, he realized what had happened. It was the old mare who had saved her master's life, and one hopes she was given an extra feed of corn when they returned to their home. No trace was ever found of the doomed men, and Henhole guards its ghastly secret to this day.

In common with many other parts of the country, Northumberland had its 'Little People' who were often mischievous, and had to be placated, otherwise the cream for the butter-making went sour, mysterious noises were heard, and spells were cast on the sheep and the cattle. Generally these 'Little People' were harmless; it was the so-called witches who suffered so greatly and were blamed when stock was ill. Accused of having the evil eye, these wretched old women often met terrible deaths by drowning. It was in the days of the great witch hunt of James I and VI that the persecution was at its worst, and many a poor innocent old woman was harried out of the village, or worse still, to her death. Possibly it was the dreaded foot-and-mouth disease, which wrought such havoc in 1966 in many parts of Northumberland, that was, in the age of superstition, the cause of outbreaks of illness amongst cattle and sheep; but the evil eye was blamed, and gruesome were the punishments meted out to the suspects.

Witchcraft was believed to have been practised at Riding Mill in Tynedale, and in Edlingham in the north of the county. The Edlingham witch however, was fortunate, as she escaped punishment, although testimony of what now appears to be the most ridiculous kind, was given against her by many people. Edlingham, so attractive and pleasant a village now, with its church built on grassy ground amid the moorlands, cannot have been a happy dwelling place for Margaret Stothard with her evil reputation.

Lorbottle, which lies close to the Roman road between High Trewhitt and Callaly, and near the road which leads over from Thropton in Coquetdale, has one of the most extraordinary legends in Northumberland. The inhabitants had the reputation of being so weak-minded, or in Northumbrian, 'sackless', that they were unable to tell when it was raining, unless they saw drops falling into a pond called 'The Puddle'. But this was the least of their limitations, as they imagined that the moon was a red cheese, and set off to haul it down with ropes!

At the nearby farm of Dancing Hall there was a colony of fairies, who one can only think bewitched their Lorbottle neighbours. Raided by the Scots in days gone by, Lorbottle also had visits from both Cavaliers and Roundheads during the Civil War, and it was here that a party of King's men were set upon by a troop of Parliamentarians under a Colonel Sanderson, and sixty Royalists and their horses perished. To quote Colonel Sanderson's report: "The first towne we fell into was Tossons, where we took a liewtenant and sixe of his dragoons in bed; the next towne was Lorbottle, where we took 60 horses and sixty men in bed."

There must have been many more inhabitants of the hamlets of Tosson and Lorbottle in the seventeenth century than now; they are both sparsely populated districts today. The ancient name of this village of sub-normal inhabitants was Lowrebotell, signifying that it is of Saxon origin. By the sixteenth century

today's spelling was used, as in the verse commemorating a
Scottish raid.

> Mark Ker rode on, and Mark Ker rode on,
> And never a hoof or horn saw he,
> Till he came to the ford of Lorbottle burn,
> Where a dainty drove lay on the lea.

No doubt the 'dainty drove' found its way into Scotland.

White ladies and grey ladies, phantom dogs and horses, all
figure in the many ballads and songs of Northumberland; cruel
sisters and wicked step-mothers are scattered over the county with
careless abandon. Ladies forsaken by their lovers still keep watch
on moonlight nights. From St Cuthbert to the Border raiders is a
far cry but it is all part of the pattern of Northumberland's history. What an achievement it would be if someone could collect
the many legends into one volume, and not as so often happens,
allow them to become forgotten tales.

It is refreshing to say farewell to the legends of this chapter
on a cheerful note, in the words of 'The Fair Flower of Northumberland'.

> They took her up beside them then,
>   Follow my love, come over the strand,
> And brought her to her father again,
>   And she the fair flower of Northumberland.

> Now all you maids be warned by me,
>   Follow no Scotsman over the strand.
> Scots never were true, nor ever will be
>   To Lord nor lady, nor fair England.

6

Boggles

I know not how the truth may be
I tell the tale as told to me.
—Scott

GHOSTS in Northumberland are known as boggles and many are
the grim stories of ghostly visitations and strange goings on in
various parts of the county.

South Tynedale has an almost inexhaustible supply of supernatural events; some of these stories have been handed down
through the centuries by word of mouth, others have been
recorded by local people and can be found in many of the village
histories. In *Haydon Bridge and District* published by William Lee
in 1876, there are accounts of several extraordinary happenings in
the district, one of the most famous being 'The Land Ends
Boggle'.

The scene of this boggle's activities was what is now called
West Land Ends Farm. Situated on rising ground on the south
side of the South Tyne, a little west of Haydon Bridge, this is
now a modern, well equipped farm on the Langley Estate of Mr
T. A. Bates, a great-nephew of C. J. Bates, the noted historian,
who was responsible for the restoration of Langley Castle. West
Land Ends today with its well-farmed land, its herd of dairy
Friesians, and cheerful house, is difficult to associate with the
eerie account of the supernatural activities which took place
there at the beginning of the last century.

According to William Lee, he heard the story from a group of
men who had gathered at the bridge end for a gossip. This was
sometime in the 1870s, and now in the 1960s men still gather at

the bridge end, but the conversation is more likely to be about football and television than boggles. Haydon Bridge is a large village which lies on both sides of the river, half way between Newcastle and Carlisle. At one time the mail coach came this way, and the Anchor Hotel on the south side of the bridge was a well-known coaching house.

At the time of the boggle's exploits, West Land Ends, or as Mr Lee calls it West Land's End, was occupied by a Mr Armstrong, who had a manservant named Oliver. An unmarried manservant was usually called 'the lad' and lived in the farm house. It was this man, Oliver, who was first tormented by the apparition. This boggle was most original in its disguises, as it was first seen in the form of a chandelier! Naturally 'the lad' was amazed to see such a form of lighting in his bedroom, and hastened to tell his master and family what he had seen. Changing its shape to avoid monotony, but never again to anything as bizarre as the chandelier, the boggle, who for some reason was given the name of Jesse, was extremely noisy, and thunderous bangs heralded his approach. Unlike many ghosts, who have usually been terrifying and destructive, Jesse was most industrious and helpful about the farm. He would harness the horses to the carts, and fill the racks with hay, but sometimes he acted in a more orthodox manner and undid all that the men had done, and scared the people who lived on the surrounding farms; he delighted in springing out from a plantation by the name of Gate's Settle, and it was practically impossible to persuade a horse to pass this plantation. Jesse had an aversion to crossing streams, so his activities were limited, and he never travelled further than the Lees burn, which runs into the Tyne west of Land Ends.

The time came when the Armstrong family decided to leave their haunted farm, and accordingly set off on a journey to the Bush Farm, which is about two miles east of Haydon Bridge where the road takes a series of sharp bends. Feeling quite sure that Jesse had been left behind, the furniture was loaded, and the journey began. All was uneventful, until someone, out of curiosity, asked the driver of the cart if Jesse had been left behind, when a voice called out from a wooden churn, "We are all going to the Bush together". Not wishing to have Jesse as a permanent member of his household, Mr Armstrong is said to have engaged the services of an old man, Jack Trumbell to 'lay' the ghost. His efforts proved successful and The Land Ends Boggle was never heard of again.

The farm of East Land Ends which is nearer to Haydon Bridge, achieved fame in a very different manner from its neighbour, as the birthplace of John Martin the artist, to whom sufficient recognition has not been given by his native village. Far more is known of a half-witted brother who gained notoriety by his attempt to set fire to York Minster.

The Martin brothers were the sons of a journeyman tanner from Hexham, who also taught 'the sword and stick exercise'. John, his third son was a self-taught artist who gained national fame; but the others were extremely peculiar—each wrote his autobiography, and William the eldest, who did not suffer from false modesty, described himself as a 'natural philosopher and conquerer of all nations'. Richard, the second son served in the Army for twenty-nine years and fancied himself as a poet. Jonathan, the youngest grew up to be a religious maniac, with a pathological hatred of the Church of England, which led to his, mercifully unsuccessful, attempt to burn York Minster. This exploit resulted in his arrest and imprisonment in Newcastle, before being removed, for his own and other's safety, to an asylum. Possibly born mentally unstable, poor Jonathan's character cannot have been improved by his experience as a press-ganged man, especially as his time was served in the Navy, under the harsh conditions of the early nineteenth century. Jesse the boggle's span was spent in pleasanter surroundings than those of his unfortunate neighbour.

A few miles west of Haydon Bridge, between Bardon Mill and Haltwhistle on the north bank of the South Tyne is the farmhouse of Hardriding, at one time a stronghold of the Ridley family. In 1933, the late Walter A. Ingledew published a small pamphlet entitled 'The Hardriding Ghost. A Strange Incident at a Bardon Mill Farm'. This pamphlet was for private circulation only. Mr Ingledew dedicated his publication to the late Mr William

Armstrong of Hardriding "In appreciation of many kindnesses covering a period of forty-five years friendship". According to Mr. Ingledew, the name is Hardriding because the original farmhouse was so thickly surrounded by trees, that its situation was almost impregnable. A date stone of the original house is inserted in the east gable of the present farm. The stone bears the inscription 'Y.Y.N.R.E. 1315'.

The story of the ghost or boggle is not an ancient one, as its first recorded appearance was as recently as 1932. There is however an earlier version of the haunter of Hardriding, which in Mr Ingledew's words is as follows:

"At midnight in the month of December, towards the latter part of that month, whilst an intruder was seeking to scale the Curtain Wall with a view to opening the Gate to permit his confederates entry within, and storming the Tower, putting to death all its occupants, then looting and departing, under cover of darkness, the alert watchman noticed the would-be alien, and felled him as he was reaching the top of the wall, he dropped to the ground, gave an agonizing yell, and died. Next morning only were his feet and hands found, wolves devouring the remainder". On the anniversary of this deed, the victim's ghost is supposed to appear. This episode occurred in the fourteenth century.

For hundreds of years the occupants of Hardriding were undisturbed by ghostly visitors, although their lives could not be described as peaceful. It was in the present century that mysterious things began to happen. Noises, there had certainly been, but these were dismissed as the creaking of old furniture, and the scrabblings of mice in the wainscot. It was on the night of Christmas 1932, when the hired 'lad', by name of Bob English (a name common in the district), was about to blow out his candle and go to bed, when the ghost or boggle became active. Thuds, screams not of this world, roused the inmates of Hardriding, and although the fastenings of all doors and windows were checked, there were no signs of a human intruder. Next morning the household looked at one another rather shamefacedly at breakfast and tried to explain away the strange happen-

ings of the night. In 1933 doors were mysteriously opened and
shut, and the writer who once spent a night in the home of her
forefathers, was relieved when morning came without any ghostly
interruptions.

Unlike the Land Ends boggle, the Hardriding ghost had none
of the helpful instincts of his fellow boggle, perhaps he had a
grudge, and not surprisingly against the watchman and the wolves
who left him only with his hands and feet.

The South and North Tynes meet at Warden Rocks, and the
united rivers, known the world over as the Tyne, flow towards
the North Sea. To those who do not know Northumberland,
the Tyne is dismissed as an industrial river; for its last ten miles
it is one of the greatest ship repairing rivers in the world, but
before that stage is reached, the Tyne is one of the most beautiful
rivers in the British Isles.

The last rural village is Wylam, spanning both sides of the
river, and the old couplet runs:

> East Heddon, West Heddon,
> Heddon-on-the-Wall,
> Harlow Hill and Horsley,
> But Wylam beats them all.

Not to be outdone by South Tynedale, the Tyne Valley has its
share of ghosts and boggles, and one of the most notorious has
its background in Whittle Dene, a stream which flows from the
Newcastle and Gateshead Water Company's Reservoir on the
Military Road.

Close to the Newcastle–Carlisle road, amidst the trees which
line the banks of the Whittle burn, are the scanty remains of a
Pele tower, which was never completed. In the reign of King
John, the royal Forester for Northumberland, a Norman baron
by the name of Philip de Ulecote, began building Nafferton Tower,
which is marked on the ordnance map as Lonkin's Hall, but
known locally as Whittle Dene Castle. On the southern side of the
Tyne, standing on an eminence which acted as a natural fortifica-
tion against attackers, is Prudhoe Castle, built by the Umfravilles.
It eventually passed into the hands of the Percy family, and now

restorations are being carried out by the Ministry of Public Building and Works.

The Lord of Prudhoe objected to the Crown against Ulecote's building operations, for which he had not received a licence, and consequently an order was issued to suspend the erection of the tower in Whittle Dene. No attempt was ever made in later reigns to finish the building and in the course of time it fell into ruin. It is however as the hide-out of a desperate character known as Long Lonkin that Nafferton Tower has attained its notoriety.

Where this character came from has never been discovered, but he soon became the terror of the district, and his ghost is reputed to haunt the dene to this day. Certainly Lonkin, 'Long' presumably from his height, was a very unpleasant character, and was accused of the murder of a woman and a child, who lived at Welton Hall near what, today is one of the reservoirs which lie on both sides of the Military Road.

In those far off days Welton was a Pele tower, part of which is incorporated in the present farm house. Lonkin was a thief in a big way, though this cannot be held against him, as most of the Northumbrians were good 'shifters'. It was the dastardly slaying of an unprotected mother and child which has given him his evil reputation. The story of Lonkin's crime is told in verse, which it is said was recited by an old woman who lived in Ovingham on the Tyne, and written down so that future generations would hold his memory in abhorrence. A serving maid at Welton is said to have been an accomplice and to have reported to Lonkin when the master of the house would be away from home.

> The Lord said to his ladie,
>   As he mounted his horse,
> "Beware of Long Lonkin
>   That lies in the moss".

> The Lord said to his ladie,
>   As he rode away,
> "Beware of Long Lonkin,
>   That lies in the clay".

Langley Castle, an almost perfect restoration

"What care I for Lonkin,
    Or any of his gang;
My doors are all shut,
    And my windows penned in."

There are six little windows,
    And they were all shut;
But one little window,
    And that was forgot.
And at that little window,
    Long Lonkin crept in.

"Where's the Lord of the Hall?"
    Says the Lonkin;
"He's gone up to London",
    Says Orange to him.

"Where's the ladies of the Hall?"
    Says Lonkin,
"They're up in their chambers",
    Says Orange to him.

"How shall we get them down?"
    Says Lonkin;
"Prick the babe in the cradle"
    Says Orange to him.

The cries of the child brought the Lady of Welton from up-stairs, when for no apparent reason Lonkin murdered both mother and child and threw their bodies into a deep pool in the nearby burn. Orange the maid-servant was presumably the accomplice. We are not told what happened when the Lord of Welton returned, and there are conflicting accounts of the end of Lonkin's horrible career. One is that he hanged himself in a fit of remorse, and another, which is much more in keeping with his character, is that he fell into the burn and was drowned. The ghost of this very nasty occupant of Nafferton Tower still haunts the scenes of his crimes, it is said to this day, or perhaps he is still searching for the treasure which he is alleged to have wrapped in

F

A Border shepherd with his collies
Judging Border Leicesters (Matthew Ridley second from right)

a bull's hide and thrown into the burn, where there is a small waterfall and a deep pool called the Whirl Dub.

The little stream the Boggle Burn, which joins the larger one of Whittle, no doubt has associations with Long Lonkin. As recently as 1891 parents threatened their children with the ghost of Lonkin should they not come home before dark. Local legend says Whittle Dene is inhabited by fairies, who perhaps by now, have driven out the evil spirit of Long Lonkin.

West of Newcastle, where the City and County of that name ends, and the County of Northumberland begins, is Denton Hall, a house built in 1622. The ghost of Denton Hall gave warning of her approach sometimes by the rustling sound of silk (which gained her the name of Silky), as did another very different type of supernatural character, also called Silky, who had her head-quarters at Black Heddon, near the village of Stamfordham. Denton Hall is surrounded by trees, and though so close to the busy main road, has an aloof appearance, as though disassociating itself from the modern world.

Silky never interfered with the family of Denton Hall; it was in the hearts of visitors that she struck terror; and many guests after a visit from Silky, who appeared in the form of a very old lady, richly dressed, her fingers covered with rings, refused to spend more than one night in the house. Silky, like many ghosts, was sometimes extremely noisy, and in addition to rustling heralded her approach with thuds and bangs, as though dragging a heavy object, which she disposed of by opening a window and casting into the night.

Thomas Doubleday recounted how a one-time visitor when she was very old, described to him her terrifying experience at Denton Hall. This old lady, then a young girl, had returned from a ball, and was sitting in her bedroom, reliving the momentous evening, during which she had met a young man who was to become her future husband. Suddenly she was aware that she was not alone; seated in an arm-chair was Silky, dressed in all her glory. Silky was not original, as her remarks to the terrified girl were a series of platitudes, the gist of it being that all that glisters is not gold. Having made these trite observations and prophesied an unhappy future for the guest, she disappeared through the door, although it was securely locked! There is a story, without much foundation, that a young girl had been strangled in the house, but whether Silky was involved or not, is not known. Naturally guests avoided the particular bedroom which held such an attraction for the Ghost of Denton Hall. This Jacobean house is one of the first to be built in the county without any provision for defence.

The Union of the Crowns had brought to an end the ceaseless Border warfare, and henceforth houses in Northumberland were built as homes and not as fortresses. A castle there may have been at Denton before the present house was built, and tradition says that in earlier times it was a summer residence of the monks of Tynemouth. Passing through the hands of various owners (including the Dentons, from whom it takes its name), it came into the possession of the well-known Northumbrian family of Errington. For a time it was the home of Edward Montagu and his gifted wife Lady Mary Wortley, who was the author of a famous collection of Letters.

Among distinguished visitors reputed to have visited Denton Hall are the artist, Sir Joshua Reynolds, David Garrick the actor, and the much travelled Doctor Johnson, who seems to have stayed at nearly every famous house in England and Scotland.

Silky of Black Heddon differed from her namesake of Denton in that although her clothes made the same type of rustling noise, she was not an upper-class ghost, but a country boggle. Her great delight was to frighten horses and riders by jumping on the back of a horse and seating herself behind the terrified rider. She cast spells over the farm horses which could only be lifted by the use of rowan berries, long regarded as a safeguard and protection against the supernatural.

At the village of Hedley on the Hill in South-east Northumberland, which crowns a range of hills which are close to the Durham Border and divide the valleys of Tyne and Derwent, there was at one time a most mischievous boggle, the Hedley Kow. He delighted in tormenting the servant girls by imitating the voices of their sweethearts, unravelling knitting, upsetting pots and pans, putting the spinning wheel out of order, and evidently the boggle with the strange name was a cat lover, as he always gave the cream to the farmhouse cat. The Hedley Kow was capable of turning himself into a truss of hay, and compelling frail old women to carry him home! For nearly a hundred years nothing had been heard of his capers, until quite recently when a man on his way to The Feathers Inn is believed to have seen the Kow.

One of the most dramatic views in Northumberland is from this village which is perched on the rim of the county. Looking north on a clear day all Northumberland is spread out like an aerial photograph, with the Cheviot in the background guarding the Border Line. At one time both coal and iron were mined in the district and ponies brought their loads down to the river Tyne. Hedley has no village hall and the local Women's Institute holds its meeting in the homes of members.

This corner of Northumberland together with parts of County Durham is hunted by the Braes of Derwent, and in 1955 Mr G. A. Cowen the Master, wrote a history of the Hunt, in which he described *A Hundred Years of Fox-Hunting in the Derwent Valley*. Many a ghostly horse and hound must haunt this country and run their quarry to earth again.

> Where the woodland runs up to the heather,
>   That blooms mid the cliffs and the rocks,
> Looking out on the fine autumn weather,
>   Sat little Red Fox.
>
> Hard by lay the vixen his mother,
>   Gazing down on the valley beneath,
> Said she; "There thy father and brother
>   Ran to meet death".
> But the cub sat and longed to discover
>   The world that from far he had seen,
> And he cried "I'll go down to the covert
>   And valley so green".
>
> Till one morn as he heard the loud holloa,
>   He said to himself in his pride,

"I am clever and fast, let them follow,
    And gallop and ride ..."

The cry of the hounds far behind him
    Came closer the farther he went,
The rain seemed to choke him and blind him
    And strengthen the scent.

Sharp stones cut his pads as he scrambled
    Up the path he had once known so well,
On the rocks where a cub he had gambolled,
    He staggered and fell.
Then strong came the sound of the horn in
    His ears as he dashed o'er the rocks,
At the mouth of the earth he was born in,
    Died little Red Fox.

So wrote a member of another Hunt, the Haydon, more than fifty years ago.

Whether or not one believes in the supernatural, there is no other county in England so rich in history and legend as Northumberland, and on lonely stretches of moorland (such as the Ottercops) it is possible to imagine, particularly under the Hunter's Moon, one can see the raiders riding the foray again.

In the Tyne and Coquet valleys, in Redesdale and on Tweedside, the history of Northumberland lives on in legend and story. Castles and Pele towers, sturdy stonebuilt farmhouses, all have their particular interest. Although this chapter has largely been concerned with the southern part of Northumberland, the tales embodied in it are typical of those found in other parts of this vast tract of country. Here, where the people have a pride in their past and a belief in their future, old tales are still repeated. The ghosts and boggles are woven into the history of the almost legendary figures of the Mosstroopers, whose careers so often ended on the gallows tree:

By Tweedside and Tyne there be kine and sheep,
Outlaw or inlaw we arl men draw breath;
As a body doth sow, sae shall he reap,
And the reiver's harvest is grim black death.

7

Farming Through the Years

General View of the Agriculture of the County of Northumberland
with
Observations on the means of its Improvement
Drawn Up For The Consideration of
The Board of Agriculture
And Internal Improvement
By J. Bailey and G. Culley
The Third Edition
"Happy Northumbria!
Grateful thy soil, and merciful thy clime,
Thy streams unfailing in the summer's drought;
Thy vallies float
With golden waves, and, on thy mountains, flocks,
Bleat numberless; while roving round their sides,
Bellowing the blackening herds in lusty droves".
1805

THIS somewhat flowery introduction to their observations by
Mr Bailey and the more famous Mr Culley contrasts sharply with
the realistic outlook farming of the highly mechanized farming
of today. The flattering references to the climate of Northumberland 'merciful thy clime' would not be the general opinion of
many, not even the most ardent Northumbrian. Winter in
Northumberland is often long drawn out, with a late spring.
Everyone rejoices when there is, in the language of the county,
'an open winter', that is to say one with very little snow.

Nevertheless, in spite of its rather ponderous style, this book
contains much valuable information on the type of farming in

Northumberland at the end of the eighteenth and the beginning of the nineteenth centuries.

Due to its situation as a Border county, and the continual fighting between England and Scotland, to say nothing of the Border raiding, Northumberland was slow in developing its agriculture potentialities. Until the Union of the Crowns there was constant unrest, and cattle and sheep were lifted from the backend until the spring. In the summer the farmers won their scanty crops of hay, the only time when there was peace in England's most northerly county.

It was not until the Enclosure Acts and the introduction of the rotation of crops that men who had formerly been raiders took to tilling their land. Farm stock was becoming a safe investment. No longer need a Northumbrian 'gentleman' pass his hand across his throat when he awoke in the morning, to make sure it had not been cut during the night!

Today some of the best farming in the United Kingdom is to be found in Northumberland. Apart from the industrial triangle which contains Tyneside, the county is purely agricultural. Although there are many great estates, there are also many farms which are owner-occupied. The type of farming varies according to the geographical layout of the land.

In the Cheviot country and the upper reaches of the valleys it is largely hill farming; in this country the sheep outnumber the people, although for reasons of economy and the shortage of shepherds some of the lowland farmers are disposing of their flocks.

In the lower reaches of the valleys, in the middle of the county and on the coastal plain it is mixed farming and stock-raising, or especially in the Alnwick district, feeding cattle. Many dairy herds are kept to supply the thickly populated areas of Tyneside.

Since the First World War farming has changed completely from a way of life to an industry. No longer is the fool of the family considered only fit for farming. The farmer of today, be he Northumbrian or not, has to be a highly skilled administrator and keep abreast of the tremendous changes which are constantly taking place.

Could John Thomson, the writer of an article which appeared in *The Scottish Leader* in 1893, return to the Tyne valley and see the farms he described in such glowing terms, he might fail to recognize them as those he visited so long ago.

The farms which he inspected were Shaw House on the Newcastle—Carlisle road between Horsley and Corbridge, Peepy, in the same district on the south side of the road, and Peel Well north of Haydon Bridge, the home of the writer's grandfather, Matthew Ridley, known as 'Mattha of the Peel Well' and to whose memory, this book is dedicated.

In his article, Thomson certainly spared neither himself nor his reader from the most trivial incident. Flowers, birds, the scenery are all described at great length. "Brambles were sterile and we did not see a single haw, nor did we notice any during our stay on Tyneside. But there was a fair show of elderberries. Rhododendrons were in bloom at Newton Hall' (now a boy's preparatory School). Very little is written about Shaw House, apart from repeating an obituary notice which had appeared in *The Newcastle Weekly Chronicle* on the death of Mr Edward Charlton who apparently was ill at the time of Thomson's visit. Throughout his article Mr Thomson used the editorial 'we'.

After a circuitous route Peepy is reached at last, but not before our Mr Thomson has waxed ecstatic over the largest crab-apple tree ever seen! In 1893 the tenant of Peepy was Mr J. K. Lyall, and the poetical Mr Thomson tells us that "Historic Peepy has long been associated in our minds with departed friends and noble shorthorns"—a curious combination! Today the name is synonymous with Friesian, the famous Hunday Herd of Messrs Moffitt. In Lyall's time heavy root crops were grown at Peepy, but surely it is a printer's error to say that *marigolds* were well stored, mangolds surely. A henhouse on wheels interested the Scottish gentleman greatly, as it could be moved from field to field after harvest and the fallen grain provided food for the poultry. Battery hens were undreamt of in 1893.

After leaving Peepy there is a description of market day at Hexham, which, as it was then, is still held on a Tuesday. The impression of the stock at Hexham was not up to the standard of praise lavished on Peepy; in fact "We saw little to admire in the white sheep, and still less in the cattle, but the blackfaced sheep pleased us greatly". The sale was conducted at Messrs Cooke & Co's Mart. Now there are two marts in Hexham, known locally as the 'High Mart' and the 'Low Mart'. After leaving Hexham the journey to Haydon Bridge was made by train, and the steep climb up 'the bank' to Peel Well began. Three times as much space is devoted to Peel Well as to any other place mentioned, and there is a character study of Matthew Ridley.

"Mr Matthew Ridley is abundant in energy, tireless in action, unbounded in enthusiasm, quick in observation, prompt in application, fertile in resource, with a keen eye to faults or virtues in matters appertaining to his business, highly methodical and intensely practical in his disposition, we were not surprised that this farm and the stock it carried far exceeded our expectations." So much praise is lavished on Peel Well that the writer wonders if the visitors had indulged in the generous hospitality for which Peel Well was famous. A great deal of this hospitality was dispensed from 'grey-hens' of whisky. These strangely named containers were stone jars cradled in wicker. The price of a 'grey-hen' would be less than a bottle is today.

A Newcastle paper reported that the cutting of the corn, was finished on August 16th 1893 being only a week later than in the dry summer of 1868. In times gone by there was a saying in the county that there was no luck in an August harvest, but as in those days the stooks stood in the fields for sometimes several weeks to dry, it would be September before the last load was led. Now, in the world of combine harvesters, no attention is paid to the old sayings, and already many have been forgotten. Mr Thomson's prose becomes even more flowery and the compliments even more numerous (was the level of the 'grey-hen' going down?) "Last season Mr Ridley had not an unsound root. We have in our years of wandering to and fro like a disturbed spirit [very appropriately worded in view of the writer's suspicions] seen many folds of cattle, but never before have we come across a large lot which pleased us so greatly ... they were simply magnificent." Then comes a description of the Peel Well flock of pedigree Border Leicester sheep for which Matthew Ridley was justly famous.

A Peel Well ram was sold at Kelso for the then enormous price of £100! This was in number 3 Ring, John Swan's of Edinburgh, where the aristocrats of the sheep world are still sold today, although in 1966, due to the catastrophic outbreak of foot and mouth disease in Northumberland, the Kelso Ram Sales were held at Ingleston near Edinburgh.

At one time Peel Well supplied cattle for the Royal farms at Windsor, and 'Mattha' affirmed that Queen Victoria's longevity was due to a diet of Peel Well beef!

It is doubtful whether this typical Northumbrian farmer of his day and generation swallowed all the flattery which appeared in *The Scottish Leader*. The few who remember 'Mattha of the Peel Well' all describe him as hard-headed and practical, with no time for people who tried to be something different from what they were. Townsmen were dismissed as 'counter-loupers' (jumpers) and those who asked silly questions, were 'gommerels'.

According to Heslop's *Glossary of Northumbrian Words* a Tindale man referred to the Ponteland district as 'goniel' or 'gommerel' country, meaning fool's country. Heslop does not say why Ponteland should have this population of fools. Certainly Matthew Ridley did not confine the designation to any particular district. Once when asked to propose a toast at The Border Union Show Dinner in The Cross Keys at Kelso, the old man, no doubt 'fit' by the time it was his turn to rise, simply said, "Mr Chairman, My Lords and Gentlemen, there've been plenty of lies told already without me telling any more" and sat down. It is not surprising that no further invitations were issued by the Society.

The stone mounting block which stood outside the stable door at Peel Well has gone. This mounting block often gave the old man the support he so badly needed after a good day at the Mart. No longer at Peel Well, or on most Northumbrian farms, do the men go back at night to 'fother' (fodder) the horses. The day of the heavy horse is over, apart from the very few breeders, such as Messrs Brown of Clifton near Morpeth, who breed Clydesdales for show purposes, and the few more conservative farmers in the

West Tyne district who, for sentimental or economic reasons, still have a pair of horses. It is the tractors, not the horses which 'lowse' at dinner times now. W. H. Ogilvie in his poem 'The Horse Trough' nostalgically paints a word picture, which brings a lump to the throat of any horse lover:

> Where the long slope ascends from the vale,
> At the turn where the roadway is steep,
> Where the tall grasses tangle and trail
> And the beech shadows whisper of sleep,
> Stands the horse-trough green-mantled in moss
> Where the horses once paused on the hill
> And came down with their tired heads a-toss
> To drink deep of the water at will.

And so to the last verse of the four,

> And it may be some lingering team
> That the years have still left on the road;
> But I think 'tis a wain of my dream
> That is heaped with old loves as a load;
> And the sound of the hoofs I have heard
> Is but sport of the winds as they pass,
> And the fern at the trough only stirred
> By some night thing that moves in the grass.

Very few of the farm workers today would tolerate the conditions under which their forbears lived in 1893 and for many years later. They worked long hours—no overtime then—for small wages and managed to rear large families. Hard master though he was, Matthew Ridley was described by his men as just; they stayed with him for years, one or two for a lifetime. He was the first farmer in the Tyne Valley to give his men a half-day; they 'lowsed' at 12 noon on Saturdays. Cottages were free, milk and eggs at a standard rate all the year round, and 'kirn' (churn) milk was free. The coals were led for the men (Northumbrians never refer to carting) and there was always a joint of meat at Christmas. Now, with the drift from the land and the increasing difficulty in getting farm labour, more and more farmers are going over to mechanization entirely, some even having given up their dairy herds, in favour of cows and sucklers, which require less labour.

Up till the outbreak of the Second World War there was a much greater family relationship between master and man than there is today. The writer remembers with love and affection many of the men who worked on her father's farms.

The country child of today misses so much: the closely knit community, the personal interest in the land and the stock, and the enjoyable but now outdated methods of transport. It is the older generation who derived so much pleasure from riding home behind a pike of hay on the horse-drawn bogies (a wagon, peculiar to the North, resembling a haywain), and sliding down those same bogies at the end of the day, even though the result was a mass of 'speiks'—as splinters are known in Northumberland —which was extremely painful. One of the great events was the Thresher Day. Soon after dark the night before, the engine pulling the threshing machine would chug its way through the yard gate, and over the cobble-stones to the stackyard. The hurricane lamps hanging on the front and back shone like great cat's eyes in the darkness. As many as twenty men would sit down to dinner on a Thresher Day. Where food was in generous supply, the farms were known as 'good meat' houses. A great round of beef was set on the long table, joints the size of which are rarely seen today, accompanied by vegetables and gravy. The main course was followed by suet puddings bulging with fruit, then after their pint pots of tea the men would go back to their work until it was time for the 'teas' to be carried out. One of Northumberland's many peculiar habits is the persistent use of the plural, especially with regard to meals. The tea was brewed and poured into large cans, and baskets were filled with home-made girdle-cakes and tea cakes spread with thick golden butter. Samples of grain were poured into little linen bags ready for the visit of the corn-merchant (no grain-driers in those days), and there was no guaranteed price for the crops. So much depended upon the weather and the resultant quality of the grain. Now, with the modern methods, there is more chance of saving crops even in a bad harvest than in those pre-war days, when farming was a way of life, and the tempo was slower.

Today a modern farm, especially a dairy farm, resembles a factory. There is very little hand milking now, and no longer in the local newspapers does the advertisement appear for "A strong girl wanted, able to milk or willing to learn. Good stripper." Stripping in this sense means that every drop of milk has been drawn from the cow's udder. There are still a few dairy farms where the cows are hand stripped after the milking machines have been used.

Milking parlours have been installed on many Northumbrian farms; surely parlour is a misnomer, as there is no rest for man nor beast in these clinically clean successors of the old fashioned byre. Now untouched by hand, the milk is collected by tankers, and it is becoming increasingly difficult to buy milk and cream in the country districts. The milking stools have disappeared, and instead of milk maids wearing 'clouty' bonnets there are glamorous young women in white overalls.

The character of the farm houses has changed, often with disastrous results. Old oak presses have gone to make way for modern streamlined furniture, the long settles have disappeared from the kitchens, and though the modern cookers are a vast improvement on the old fireplaces, the twentieth-century furniture is incongruous in a farm house.

Some of the grandfather clocks with the painted dials made by John Bell of Hexham have survived, though many have found their way to the antique shops which have sprung up like mushrooms in the last few years. In some cases it is the despised townspeople who have more appreciation of old and beautiful furniture than the countryman. The structure of the houses too has suffered by so called improvements. The old windows have been taken out, glass doors have replaced the solid oak, and the china dogs thrown out by the cottage people are now collected, and bring high prices in the antique shops.

During the days of the window tax, many farm houses had a cheese room, its window having the purpose engraved on the glass, thus avoiding the tax.

The 'big' farmers of a hundred years or so ago in Northumberland lived well, as the treasures, which have been handed down in families, prove. Georgian silver, exquisite china and hand woven linen were part of the prosperous farmer's way of life. In Northumberland, the farmer's children were well educated, the women skilled in needlework, quilting and sewing.

For a small working farmer, such as was to be found in the Allendale district it was a hard life, but for men such as Matthew Ridley, and there were many like him, it was a good life. The pattern of living was formed by the seasons. In the backend the cattle, apart from the outliers, were housed for the winter, the root crops were stored and there was plenty of winter 'keep'. In the long winters of Northumberland the houses were lighted by oil lamps, and the candles were made at home. Flour chests or 'kists' were filled and no panics occurred, as do now, if there is a hard winter.

Now, if a village is cut off during a snow storm, after a few days, supplies have to be dropped by helicopter. The farmers of the past were self-supporting and far seeing; they made their plans in advance, and laid in their stores of food. In the spring, after the lambing storm (usually in mid-March) the in-bye lambing began; to be followed later by the out-bye flocks. Very much the same cycle is carried out today, in the summer the store lambs are fattened, followed by the many Sales which are held all over Northumberland in the autumn.

It is in the haytime and the harvest that the most revolutionary changes have taken place. The 'kyles' (small hay-cocks) and 'pikes' have disappeared from the fields to be replaced by bales. In the days when the men forked the hay to build up the 'pike', towards the end of the proceedings, one man would stand on top of the pike to poss down the hay. 'Poss' is a word rarely used today, but it expresses exactly what the process is, far better than the 'English' version of beating. The country-side will never seem quite the same now that the tall 'pikes' have disappeared. It is only in the Highlands and more remote places that they survive, and unlike the Northumbrian 'pike' which is solid hay, the Scottish 'pike' is spread over a wooden tripod for the purpose of drying the hay more quickly.

In the harvest time now the farm worker no longer has the

back-breaking task of gathering the sheaves as they dropped from the binder and building them into stooks, nor are the sheaves led home in the 'long' cart. Yet with all the progress that has been made, in a wet harvest the machines become bogged down, and sometimes when the corn is laid it has to be cut one way.

Northumberland has many sporting farmers, who either shoot or hunt with the many packs of hounds which are in the county. Light horses and hunters still abound in Northumberland, and pony clubs flourish. Those who shoot are described by the old people as the 'shutters', and those who hunt 'gan' after the huns' (hounds).

Northumberland is not a tourist county. There are so many big estates and well farmed land which keep the population employed. In fact the average countryman, though intensely proud of his county, does not always welcome the visitor, who sad to say, often has no idea of how to behave on other people's land.

The way of life which has become an industry is very much a closed shop, farmers are inclined to stick together, and their inevitable subject of conversation is farming. At a dispersal sale of farm stock, every type of farmer can be encountered, some come to buy, but many come out of curiosity to see what the 'place' is like, if the buildings have been improved, and if possible to have a look inside the house. A farm to let is at a premium, and those young men who manage to get to the top list of would-be tenants count themselves extremely fortunate.

The modern Northumbrian farmer is a worthy successor of his forebears who, after the raiding days were over, settled down to till their land and raise their stock and put Northumberland on the farming map.

Long ago when the land was still poor men struggled to make a living out of the earth they loved, and to use another local expression it 'got over'. A poem by Hedworth Williamson, 'A Northern Headstone' sums up the life of a small farmer of those days:

Strong with its stunted tower, gray in the driving shower,
Stands the old Church with the moors for a setting.
Under the turfy heap my old friend sleeps his sleep,
Lichen and sea wind the headstone are fretting.
What did he do with his life? Tended an ailing wife,
Buttressed the bridge and rebuilt the byre,
Drained the five acre field, doubled the yearly yield,
Tiled the west gable-end after the fire.
Drought in the early spring, rain in the harvesting.
Even a good season's niggardly bounty
All his life long he knew, yet oats like his were few,
And his swedes famous this side the county.
Now his day's work is done, night begun, resting won.
He lies so quietly under the clover,
Heeds not the rain and wind, this world well left behind,
Good times and bad times, and all times got over.

A fitting epitaph for all countrymen.

Although the world of agriculture has changed fundamentally the farmers are very much the same as they were in the old days. The greatest pleasure of a farmer's life is to drive out in his car on a Sunday afternoon (to be driven by a farmer is hazardous, as they are so intent on seeing what is going on around them that they usually drive with their heads poking out of the window). Not very much is said during the drive but on returning, as a Northumbrian farmer drives into his yard, before getting out of his car, he draws himself up and says, "Well I shouldn't say it, but I haven't seen any farming better than my own".

8

Rock Township

The Lord is my shepherd; I shall not want.
He maketh me to lie down in green pastures:
He leadeth me beside the still waters.
                              —Twenty-third Psalm.

ROCK village or, as it is described in the County History, township is one of the most attractive villages in the north-east of the county. Built on an outcrop of limestone, from which the origin of its name is obvious and situated between the Great North Road and the sea, where Northumberland narrows towards the apex of its triangle, Rock deserves a chapter to itself.

In 1965 when the National Federation of Women's Institutes held their competition for the best scrap-book describing village life as it is today, Rock and South Charlton was awarded a special prize for the best entry from a small Institute in Northumberland. This was all the more meritorious as the membership is only twenty-eight. In the scrap-book the life of the inhabitants of Rock is graphically portrayed, and it is regrettable that so few people can have the opportunity of seeing and reading this beautifully produced record. No detail has been omitted from this comprehensive survey of village life in the Northumberland of the 1960s. The number of the population, their occupations, the type of houses in which they live, the social life of the village, and the smallest detail of what is largely an agricultural community, are all dealt with in the most descriptive language. Photographs are included, and even pieces of dress materials, furnishing fabrics, and of wallpaper, so that future generations will have tangible evidence of how their parents and grand-parents lived.

G

The Parish extends to 2,100 acres, and has for eight centuries been in undivided ownership—from William de Rok to the Bosanquets. Today in 1968 three farms are let to Rock Farms Limited, in which the principal shareholders are members of the Bosanquet family, and three farms are let to individual tenants. The present head of this family of Huguenot extraction, who lives at Rock Moor House, is Mr C. I. C. Bosanquet, who was the first Vice-Chancellor of Newcastle University.

By the coming of the Bosanquets to Northumberland, the village of Rock and the estate underwent a transformation. Prior to that time Rock and the surrounding district was for the most part unenclosed moorland; in fact most of the land north of Alnwick was treeless and barren. This is difficult to imagine today, as this part of Northumberland is now not only picturesque, but produces some of the best farming in a county famous for its good husbandry.

The story of this now delightful 'township' is the all too familiar one in this once lawless land. It is a story of neglected estates, their owners preferring fighting to farming; in fact the Northumbrians of days gone by were always spoiling for a fight, either against their neighbours, with whom they seem to have been often literally at daggers drawn, or against their hereditary enemies, the Scots.

When William Cobbett visited Alnwick in October 1832 his description was not complimentary. "From Morpeth to this place [Alnwick] the country generally speaking, is very poor land, scarcely any trees at all; the farms enormously extensive, only two churches, I think, in the whole of the twenty miles; scarcely anything worthy of the name of a tree, and not one single dwelling having the appearance of a labourer's house.

"Here appears neither hedging nor ditching, no such thing as a sheep fold or a hurdle to be seen; the cattle and sheep very few in number, the farm servants living in the farm houses, and very few of them, the threshing done by machinery and horses, a country without people."

Could the same gentleman come back today he would no doubt form a very different impression of 'this place' and its surroundings. Perhaps Cobbett did not realise what life in a Border county had been like, when it was the survival of the fittest, and every man for himself. The story of Rock is an example which can be duplicated in many parts of the county.

Formerly part of the Barony of Alnwick, Rock was held in the reign of Henry II by a William de Rok: "For half a knight's fee of ancient feoffment". The occupation of Rock by this family was brief, as their name soon ceases to appear in any records. The wealthiest man in the township was a John de Cambo, whose name is on the Subsidy Roll for 1296 against the amount of £4. 8s. od.!

After the passing of the Roks, the Tuggals came, and their name is perpetuated in the nearby Tuggal Hall. Scremerston, south of Berwick, was also Tuggal property where, as at Rock, there was an oratory. In the year 1359 Robert de Tuggal applied to Bishop Hatfield (the Bishop, after whom one of the colleges of Durham University is named) to have services performed in 'his oratories at Rock and Scremerston'.

Like their predecessors, the Roks, the Tuggal ownership of their properties was short, as in the late fourteenth century, the estates passed by marriage to the Swinhoe family, who possibly took their name from the hamlet of the same name on the road from Chathill to Seahouses.

The Tower which stands today was probably built on the site of an earlier stronghold. As is the case with many of the fortified dwellings of Northumberland alterations were carried out during the centuries. Many of the additions at Rock Hall, as it is called now, date from Elizabethan days. Severely damaged by fire in 1752, the house was in a ruinous condition until its restoration by Charles Bosanquet in 1819. Now, no longer occupied by the family, Rock Hall is a Youth Hostel.

Long before the disastrous fire of 1752 there were many different families in possession of Rock. From the Swinhoes it again passed by marriage, this time to a Yorkshire family named Lawson, and thereafter to the Salkelds, one of whom began the building of Mid Hall which was demolished in 1855. The most colourful character, and the most notorious of these was a Colonel Salkeld, son of the Mid Hall builder, whose memorial can be seen in Rock Church today. The epitaph is rather surprising, as one of his many exploits was anything but admirable.

According to the fulsome wording of the epitaph, "He served King Charles ye I st with a constant, dangerous, and expensive loyalty as volunteer, captain and collonell of horse; and for his service of his king and country, he took in Berwick-upon-Tweed and Carlisle, which was a rice [rise] to the war of '48. He afterwards served in Ireland under King Charles and King James ye 2nd. as Lieutenant-Col. He was Justice of ye Peace 35 years, and aged 89; departed this life June the 2nd 1705."

Nothing is mentioned about this magistrate's criminal assault on a Swinburne of Capheaton, whom he deliberately murdered near the gates of Meldon Hall. Salkeld avoided his just retribution by escaping to another county. He came back to Northumberland five years later as though nothing had happened!

A contemporary account is quoted in the *County History*: "On 13th February 1643, a coroner's jury reported that 'upon the thirteenth day of February in the eighteenth year of our Sovereign Lord, King Charles, about three of the clocke in the afternoon of the same day, Captain John Salkeld of Rock did, out of premeditated malice, assault Mr John Swynburn of Capheaton, gent, at a place nigh unto Meldon-gates, and with a rapier sword in his right hand to the value of five shillings sterlinge, did then and there give unto John Swynburn one mortal wound in the right side of his belly of the depth of an inch or two, and in breadth about an inch, of which mortall wound John Swynburn did languish, and languishing, lived from the aforesaid day until the fifteenth day of the said month of February, being Wednesday, and then and there, at Meldon, John Swynburn died about three of the clocke in the forenoone; and thus wee find Mr John Swynburn to be wilfully murdered by Captain John Salkeld. The evidence of a witness shows that the murderer received no provocation, and was probably intoxicated at the time. Henry Brown deposeth that he was present with others at Meldon when Mr Swynburn was slane by Mr Salkeld. Mr Swynburn being riding upon his hors at Meldon Gaits, intending to ride home after his wife who had gone a little before to Capheaton, Salkeld stept after him and would have him light and drinke more. Mr Swynburn refused. Salkeld told him he should light and drink a cup more; but still Mr Swynburn refused, whereupon Salkeld stept afore him and drew his rapier, made a thrust at him and hurt his horse; whereupon Mr Swynburn seeing his hors hurt, alighted, and as he was letting his cloike fall from him, prefering to lay his hand on his sword, whereupon I being present and his servant, run in hastily, fearing my master Mr Swynburn should have drawn his sword.

" 'I cacht hold of him, and in ye intrem Salkeld came running in and thrust him in the belly, which wound was his death'."

From this rather confused account of the tragedy at Meldon 'Gaits'—the variations in the spelling appear in the original—it is difficult to reconstruct what actually happened. Of one thing there is no doubt, drunk or sober, the future Justice of the Peace was a murderer. Did Swinburne's relatives (using the present day spelling of the name) make no effort to prevent Salkeld's escape, and when the gallant Colonel eventually returned to his native county, to fight for the Royalist cause, what were relations between Rock and Capheaton?

In 1701, a Fenwick of Rock was executed for the murder of a Forster during a duel in Newcastle's Newgate Street. Surely more leniency should have been shown to killing as the result of duelling which was then legal, than a deliberate murder such as that of John Swinburne.

After the Treaty of Union, Rock saw many changes, as life in Northumberland was gradually becoming more peaceful and the turf built houses were replaced by stone with stone roofs, many years afterwards replaced by tiles.

Even so this must have been slow progress, as, almost a hundred years after the death of Colonel Salkeld a survey of the church reported that, "They want the new Communion Book and the windows of the chapel are in decay" and in 1732, there was an even worse account: "The chapell out of repair in the roof; the walls within dirty, the pulpit and reading desk in a dark and wrong situation, and the churchyard walls ruined and fenceless".

Again by marriage the estate changed hands, and became the property of the Proctor family, who were soon in financial difficulties. In 1732, Rock estate, now heavily mortgaged, was sold to Lord Jersey, an absentee land owner who had bought it as a mineral speculation, and sadly neglected the property. What a relief it must have been when, in 1794, a Mr Peter Holford bought the estate and his son Robert, in 1804, gave his Northern property to a Bosanquet, who had married his sister, the estate being in lieu of a dowry. So at long last Rock was to be improved, and in the ensuing years became the pleasant, peaceful place it is today.

During the religious persecutions in France, many Huguenot families sought refuge in England, among them the Bosanquets. The founder of the English branch of the family was David who came to London in 1686 after the Edict of Nantes was revoked.

The Story of the Bosanquets by Grace Lawless Lee, Late Fellow and Research Assistant of the Huguenot Society of London, was published in 1966, and makes fascinating reading for those who are interested in the integration into a new environment of a remarkable and distinguished family, who were prepared to leave their own country rather than give up their faith. In the case of the Bosanquets it was France's loss, and ultimately Northumberland's gain. David Bosanquet lost no time in becoming a naturalized Englishman, and branches of the family are now scattered all over the world.

Improvements to Rock church began about 1806, and each generation has carried on the task of making Rock a model estate. After the restoration of the church by Salvin, a north aisle was added in 1866; the architect in this case was F. R. Wilson. Situated between the Hall and the village, the church is surrounded by magnificent trees, planted in the early eighteenth century by the Proctors. The most striking relic of Norman times, in this much restored church, is the west doorway which is richly decorated. As the Bosanquets have been at Rock longer than any of its previous owners, there are, as is to be expected, many memorials to the family, and it is worth quoting in full the inscription of the north side of the chancel. Unlike the curious wording of

Colonel Salkeld's epitaph, it tells the true story of the first 'Northumbrian' Bosanquet's life and qualities:

"To the memory of Charles Bosanquet of Hampstead, in Middlesex, and of Rock, second son of Samuel Bosanquet of Forest house in the county of Essex, esquire, and of Eleanor, his wife, daughter of Henry Lannoy Hunter of Beechill in the county of Berkshire, esquire; born 1769; married in 1796 Charlotte Anne Holford, daughter of Peter Holford of Westonbirt in the county of Gloucester, esquire. Her monument is in this church.

"He was many years governor of the South Sea Company; as governor of the Canada Land Company he was instrumental in bringing into cultivation vast tracts of land in Canada west; he was yet more extensively known as colonel of the Light Horse Volunteers of London and Westminster; after the peace of 1815 he for some years fulfilled the duties of a commissioner of military inquiry; he also, for a considerable space of time, filled the chair of the Exchequer Loan Commission. These various occupations did not cause him to neglect his landed estate at Rock, nor to forget the interests, temporal and spiritual, of those who dwelt upon it; he completed the estate into farms; he restored the church which he found in a ruinous state; rebuilt the village and repaired and added to the old mansion, which, having been destroyed by fire, had lain in ruins for about seventy years; finally he became resident at Rock with his family, and having survived his wife for a space of eleven years, he departed this life on the 20th of June, 1850."

A very different career from that of the ardent supporter of Charles I!

Rock can claim to have royal connections, as it was on Rock Moor that the unfortunate King Charles encamped with his army during the Civil War. A print showing a plan of the camp is in the possession of the Bosanquet family today. No doubt the Cavaliers found the Moor of those days a barren waste, and as their bitter enemy Cromwell was also in Northumberland, their stay cannot have been a happy one. For once there is no mention of the Cromwellian army stabling their horses in any of the local churches. It has so often been reputed that the man who was to become Lord Protector committed this sacrilege (and there is evidence that he did so in Durham Cathedral) that the tale, like that of Queen Elizabeth I and her numerous resting places, has become legendary.

More than two hundred years after the strife of the Civil War, a Bosanquet gave an organ to Rock church, and many times on this organ will have been played the tune to which Oliver Cromwell's Ironsides marched, 'The Old Hundred', associated now with the familiar hymn, 'All people that on earth do dwell'.

Certainly for more than a century now the people of Rock have had cause to rejoice that their lives have been spent in such rural and charming surroundings. The lime trees, planted so long ago, have reached maturity; the horse-chestnuts, sycamores and the ash, which has always, according to the folk song 'flourished in the North Countree', are a memorial to the Proctor family, who not only enriched the scenery by doing so, but laid out a garden which was famous in 1704. This date together with the name and address of this family who spent such a brief period at Rock, is in a glass bottle, which is now in the possession of the present owner's family.

The couplet runs:

> Rock gardens would please Epicurus grace,
> Brave Salkeld's once, Now Proctor's place.

Why the writer thought Epicurus, a Greek philosopher, should have been interested in a Northumbrian garden, is not explained, neither is the reason given for the application of the adjective 'brave' to the notorious member of the Salkeld family! The main object of these anonymous writers seems to have been to get words to rhyme, and let the facts take care of themselves.

Famous in the eighteenth century for its gardens, a different type of fame made its name a celebrated one in the farming world, when Rock Estate became the first in the United Kingdom to have a registered flock of pedigree Border Leicester sheep. It was in 1849 that this now famous flock was founded, and to quote from a booklet entitled 'Border Leicester Sheep. Their Origin, Characteristics, and Commercial Utility', published by the

Society of Border Leicester Sheep Breeders, the Rock flock "contains the noted strain built up at Newlands, near Belford, late in the eighteenth century by Mr John Dinning, a friend and contemporary of Bakewell and the brothers Colling". This booklet goes on to say that the Rock Border Leicesters are reared upon "high limestone pastures between the Chillingham moors and the sea, a few miles north of Alnwick . . . The pick of the shearlings, fifty or sixty in number, have been sold at Kelso Ram sales since 1855." The information in this publication dates from 1921 and even now in 1968 there is still a pedigree flock at Rock.

The writer makes no apology for devoting so much space and detail to this breed of sheep; Border Leicesters seem to be aware of their long pedigree, and, if sheep can be said to have expressive features, then these well bred creatures have. Looking down their long aristocratic noses, they give the impression of despising all other breeds, except perhaps the indigenous Cheviots of Northumberland, with whom they have such a close connection. A Border Leicester ram and a Cheviot ewe produce the well known 'halfbreds' which are so numerous in the county.

There are no doubts about the 'family tree' of the Border Leicesters; they are lineal descendants of the Dishley Leicesters of Dishley, in the county from which the second part of their name is derived. Robert Bakewell, who did so much to advance the improvement of livestock, which in the course of years has made this branch of British farming supreme, was born in 1726, and died in the year 1795. The connection formed between what were then simply called Leicesters, and the Borders of England and Scotland, was the result of a visit to Dishley by Robert and Charles Colling who farmed near Darlington in the County of Durham. The fame of Bakewell's experiments had spread far beyond the boundaries of his own county, and on their return to the north the Colling brothers began to apply this Midland breeder's methods to their own flocks. Not only did this enterprising pair experiment with sheep; they applied the same methods to their cattle, and ultimately became the founders of the Shorthorn breed, at one time so numerous in the Northern counties, but now outnumbered by British Friesians.

Another pair of famous brothers who did so much for livestock breeding were Matthew and George Culley, who were
pupils of Bakewell and started farming in Northumberland in
1767. The Culley brothers brought the Leicesters to Northumberland, and as the breed began to spread into Scotland, the name
which made them famous as 'Border Leicesters' was evolved.

In 1898 the breeders formed a society, calling themselves the
Society of Border Leicester Sheep Breeders. Flock books were
issued, in which rams (or 'tups' as they are referred to in Northumberland and Southern Scotland) and ewes, were registered in-
dividually, so the Border Leicesters' owners can always refer those
who are interested in family pedigrees, to the flock books.

The Border Leicesters are also successfully crossed with other
breeds, notably the Blackface, and Suffolks, the former producing
lambs, called mules in Northumberland and Southern Scotland,
which must be most puzzling for those who are not conversant
with the terms used in the sheep world. Half-bred ewes are ex-
ceedingly good mothers, and rear strong sturdy lambs. It is
strange that a county once notorious for sheep stealing is now
famous for its pedigree flocks!

In many parts of Northumberland are road signs bearing the
warning 'Beware of Sheep'. Thousands of acres of moorland are
unfenced, and it is sad to say that numbers of ewes and lambs are
killed by careless motorists. Those who feed sheep with tit-bits
from their picnic baskets are culpable, as this encourages the
sheep to stray on to the busy roads especially at weekends. Even
where the fields are fenced, sheep seem to prefer 'the other side',
and lambs are expert in finding holes through which they can
wriggle. It is a regrettable fact that many townspeople regard the
country as a playground, in which they can do as they please:
gates are left open and dogs are allowed to chase stock, which in
the lambing season can result in premature or dead offspring. It
is not surprising that the landowners and farmers secure the
gates on their land.

Some readers may think it peculiar that the pedigree of sheep
has been given pride of place, before that of a family, especially
as that family are the owners of Rock, but those who understand

the world of pure-bred stock, will realize the pride which a successful breeder takes in his flock or herd. The writer can remember, when she was a small child, the atmosphere of excitement which preceded the Kelso Ram Sales. In those days the rams were transported by rail from Haydon Bridge, where she was born, and so precious were these animals, that they were guarded at night, as race horses are today. To 'top' number three ring on the sale ground, with its beautiful setting by the river Tweed, is an achievement to which every sheep breeder aspires.

The history of a family is fascinating: the beginnings, the background, which have all contributed to the characteristics of its members, their diversity of interests, as in the case of the Bosanquets, can be taken as the prototype of so many families.

England through the centuries has been the refuge for many persecuted races, which, with few exceptions, have contributed to the well-being of their adopted country. Ironical as it may seem, the intolerance of religious beliefs has been the chief reason for the introduction of alien blood into this small island. Had the Huguenots not been so persecuted, Northumberland would never have heard of this family, which has distinguished itself in so many ways.

This then, is the story of Rock and its several owners, all of whom in their various ways have contributed so much to the history of the County. When another volume of the County History is written a record of Rock's place in Northumberland's story should be included.

Rock is now a delight, not only for those who live there, but for those who visit it. The attractive rows of cottages with their well kept gardens, the church which is obviously loved by its parishioners, and the famous flock of Border Leicesters make Rock one of the most interesting villages in Northumberland.

The impact of the twentieth century is evident even here, and an 'architect' designed house has made its appearance. This writer finds the ideas of Town and Country Planning difficult to understand. It is left to the history of the years ahead for the verdict of what, at least to many people, is the desecration of villages, in Northumberland and throughout the United Kingdom.

Rock, like its name, is the epitome of continuity; it is part of the pattern of Northumbrian history. It is not a dying village, as so many are while the drift from the land continues; it is alive, and to use a rather overrated expression of the time 'with it'.

De Roks, Tuggals, Swinhoes, Lawsons, Salkelds, Proctors, and for a short time, the Earl of Jersey, were owners of this Northumbrian estate. Now Rock will be remembered as the home of Newcastle University's first Vice-Chancellor.

9

Contrasts in Villages

The crowning county of England—yes, the best . . .
Have you and I, then, raced across its moors
Till horse and boy were well-nigh mad with glee
So often, summer and winter, home from school,
And not found that out? Take the streams away
The country would be sweeter than the south
Anywhere: give the south our streams, would it
Be fit to match our borders? Flower and crag,
Burnside and boulder, heather and whin—you don't
Dream you can match them south of this? And then
If all the unwater'd country were as flat
As the Eton playing fields, give it back our burns,
And set them singing through a sad south world
And try to make them dismal as its fens,—
They won't be.

$\qquad$ —Algernon Charles Swinburne

THE villages of Northumberland differ as much in appearance
and character as does the county's scenery. Each village and
hamlet has its own particular individuality, its own history, and
in several cases a connection with old Northumbrian families.
There could scarcely be greater contrasts than the Kirks and
Heatons. Kirkwhelpington, through which the Wansbeck flows,
and Kirkharle, with its church standing in a field, are entirely
different from Kirkheaton with its houses built round the village
green; and Capheaton, a model village with its Hall dating from
the seventeenth century, is completely different from the township of Rock.

The reason for the prefix 'Kirk' is obvious, as both the

Northumbrians and the Scots refer to a church by this name, which is of Scandinavian derivation. It is more difficult to trace what is the meaning of Heaton, although many theories have been advanced; one suburb of the City of Newcastle is named Heaton.

Kirkwhelpington lies just off the Jedburgh road, which leaves Northumberland at the Carter Bar. Part of the village, including the church, is built on high exposed ground set amidst moorland, while the rest of the stone-built houses and cottages stand on the low ground fringing the banks of the Wansbeck, which rises not far away, and is still, at Kirkwhelpington, more a burn than a river. The most attractive approach to this historic village, is by the road from Cambo, which follows the river in its course upstream. One of the present day delights of this village is the garden of Whitridge House, which has only come into its present glory in the last four years. A stream, crossed by a little bridge adds to its charm, and the rock plants are a blaze of colour. The stream flows from one of the many springs which abound to the north of the village. Some of the local residents complained when piped water supplies came, as they were quite satisfied with the clear spring water.

As in many other places, there are new houses in Kirkwhelpington, some of them not in keeping with the design of the original plan—that is if there was a plan for these isolated villages. They were more likely to grow as the population demanded, and perhaps happily, there was no town and country planning in days gone by.

In the mid 1850s a writer tells us that the "salubrity of the atmosphere in this part of the country is much celebrated, and instances of longevity are not uncommon". In spring and summer this may have been so, but when winter comes, and the road to the Carter is blocked with snow drifts, the writer was surely using poetic licence when he used the term 'salubrious'.

Kirkwhelpington has a long history. In the reign of King John, a member of the Umfraville family "made his whole court" where now people from the cities come to their weekend cottages for peace and quiet. The de Whelpingtun's, to use the old form of spelling, do not seem to have made much contribution to the history of their county. After 1438 there is no mention of this unusual name, although in 1435, and the year 1438, Robert de Whelpingtun was Mayor of Newcastle.

The church of St Bartholemew is surprisingly large for such a small community, but it no doubt served a wider area in its earlier days. When Kirkwhelpington Church was actually built is open to conjecture, as so many relics of different periods have been found. The church contains the interesting tomb of one Gawen Aynsley, who died in 1750, and of his wife Mary. No doubt the Aynsleys were an admirable couple, but one cannot help wondering if the fulsome inscriptions, so beloved of our forefathers, were always accurate. Could human beings possibly have so many virtues? The Aynsleys were attributed to be:

Kind to their children.
Humane to their servants.
Obliging to their neighbours.
Friendly, just and courteous to all.
Religious without superstition.
Charitable without ostentation.
Lovers and practisers of virtue.

In other words, an example and a credit to the people of their parish.

It was at Kirkwhelpington that the Reverend John Hodgson, while he was Vicar there wrote most of his contribution to *The County History of Northumberland*. In 1823 Hodgson left, to become Vicar of Hartburn, where he is buried. Was his early death (he was only in his early sixties when he died) the result of the arduous research and labour which this remarkable man contributed to the writing of the history of Northumberland?

So many travellers miss the interesting village where this historian was at one time Vicar. They rush on through Knowesgate on their mad dash to cross the Border. It is well worth while to turn off to Kirkwhelpington, to wander by the banks of the infant Wansbeck, to explore the church, and follow the many by-ways which radiate from this focal point.

In 1884, according to the *Directory of Northumberland*, there was a Presbyterian Manse at nearby Great Bavington, where the Reverend Alexander Forsyth established 'a very superior school', and (to quote) "a neat Manse is in the course of erection". This is not surprising as this district is so close to the Border.

At the same time as Mr Forsyth had established his 'superior' school, the following trades employed the local people; Jacob Carr was a mason, Thomas Finling, a shoemaker, and the farmers were Thomas Helmsley, of New Housetead; Simon Lamb, of Clay Walls; William Stephenson and Richard Weddle of Campwell. In those days the parish consisted of 13,351 acres, and a population of 679 'souls'. How sure the Victorians were of immortality!

A little south of Kirkwhelpington, within sight of the main road, is Kirkharle Church, which is dedicated to St Wilfrid, who was responsible for the building of Hexham Abbey, and was at one time Bishop of York. The church is a prominent landmark, standing as it does in an isolated position in a field. The church of Kirkharle has to be approached more or less through a farm yard and there are only two houses near the church. The living is now held in plurality with Cambo. The hamlet of Kirkharle is famous as the birthplace of the celebrated landscape gardener, 'Capability' Brown. It is remarkable that there is no memorial to this boy, who, educated in the village school at Cambo, became one of the county's most famous sons, and in later years was instrumental in laying out the gardens of Blenheim Palace.

From about 1430, until 1834, Kirkharle was the home of the family of Loraine, or Lorraine as it is sometimes spelt. The old Manor House, now a farm, to the south-east of the church, was inhabited in 1381 by Alan del Strother, who is mentioned in Chaucer's *Reeves Tale*, as being a not very desirable person! This 'undesirable person' left three daughters, one of whom, Johanna, married a Loraine. Before the days of the del Strothers and the Loraines there is evidence of a church at Kirkharle. In 1350, the name of the first Vicar is recorded. Little trace of the original building remains; it was quite possibly destroyed in one of the many Border raids. The pedigree of the Loraine family

Rock village today
Rock Township's church

Countess (and) Heiress of Darwentwater. 7 October 1869. Dilstone Castle goes back into the mists of time. One of the many families which came to England in the train of William the Conquerer, this family traces its descent from the Emperor Charlemagne, the first of the Holy Roman Emperors, who reigned about A.D. 800. At his death the empire was divided between three sons, one of whom was Lothair, the name which eventually became Loraine.

There are no reasons given why this ancient family chose to come to Northumberland, a most unruly part of the conquered kingdom to select. One member of the family, Walcher, was appointed Bishop of Durham (this Bishopric then extended from the Tees to the Tweed), and later was created Earl of Northumberland. He, like del Strother, whose daughter had married a Loraine, appears to have had a not very 'desirable' character. The deputies appointed by this Bishop-cum-Earl, carried out such atrocities, one presumes by his orders, that the people demanded an enquiry. Walcher agreed to an investigation being held, and this took place at Gateshead on the Durham side of the river Tyne. Those who led the petition of complaints were not satisfied with the Prelate's replies, and launched an attack on Walcher and his retinue. Fleeing to St Mary's Church for sanctuary, the Bishop and his henchmen were literally burnt out. The outraged Northumbrians killed His Lordship on the steps of the church as he attempted to escape from the burning building. The monks of Jarrow, who were evidently supporters of Loraine's policies, buried his body in Durham Cathedral.

Another member of the family became a Bishop, but he appears to have been more humane than his kinsman, and there are no records of a violent death. There is, however, an account, which can be read in Burke's *Peerage, Baronetage and Knightage*, of the horrible end of one Robert Loraine in 1483. This barbarous deed took place close to the church, and in later years a descendant of the murdered man erected a stone, bearing an inscription which can still be seen, although the original stone was replaced in 1728. The inscription reads as follows:

"This new stone was set up in place of the old one by Sir William Lorraine, Bart, in 1728, in memory of Robert Lorraine,

H

Countess Amelia in the home of her 'ancestors'

his ancestor, who was barbarously murdered by the Scots in 1483, for his good services to his country against their thefts and robbery, as he was returning from the church alone, where he had been at his private devotions".

Burke's *Peerage* gives a much more lurid description of Robert Loraine's death, saying; "He became so formidable to the marauders upon the borders, that a party of them waylaid him returning from church in 1483, and having barbarously murdered him, cut his body into small pieces, to fulfil of cutting him into pieces small as flesh for the pot".

Expectation of life was limited in Northumberland in the centuries that preceded the Union of the Crowns, and certainly the Loraines seem to have had their fair share of violent and premature deaths. A memorial within St Wilfrid's Church extols the virtues of an eighteenth-century member of this ancient family, who died at the early age of 38, while walking in a field. As was usual in those days, no details of his illness, or the cause of death are omitted! Richard Loraine's epitaph (the spelling of the name is rarely consistent) reads as follows; "Here lys the body of Richard Loraine, Esq; who was a proper handsome man of good sense and behaviour; he dy'd a batcheler of an appoplexy walking in a green field near London, October 26th, 1738, in the 38 year of his age".

After the Glorious Restoration the first Loraine baronetcy was created by Charles II in 1664. It continued until 1961, when by the death of Sir Percy Loraine, who left no heir, like many old families, the title died out. The last of the Loraine's Northumbrian estates have been sold, for not only was it in the Kirkharle part of the county that these descendants of Charlemagne owned land, they were at one time owners of Styford Hall near Corbridge on the Tyne. Sir Percy was the twelfth baronet and his memorial is the last one to have been placed in Kirkharle Church. He made the Diplomatic Service his career, and spent very little time in Northumberland. Born in 1880, his epitaph is striking in its simplicity; "His active life was spent in the service of his country. He feared only his God. He was true to his King".

As at the time of his death, Queen Elizabeth had reigned for nine years, it might have been more appropriate to substitute 'Sovereign' for 'King', which would then have included all the sovereigns Sir Percy had served. Keenly interested in racing, Sir Percy Loraine owned Coup de Roi, the winner of the Northumberland Plate in 1936. Kirkharle has a connection with the Swinburne family of Capheaton, as the curate in charge from 1839 to 1856, acted for a time as tutor to Algernon Charles Swinburne, the poet. He spent his holidays at Capheaton, and was obviously influenced by the Northumbrian scenery, as the county is often mentioned in his verse.

The font in St Wilfrid's 'Kirk' was originally in All Saint's in Newcastle. Kirkharle Church, or rather the fabric, seems to breathe history. Rarely visited, it is one of the most rewarding small churches to explore, even in a county which can boast of so many well preserved and maintained churches. Northumberland has redeemed the terrible reputation which it had in the past, when so many visitors reported that "the churches were in a scandalously ruinous condition".

On the north side of the road to the Border and practically hidden by trees, is another of the county's many towers, Little Harle, the home of Major G. D. Anderson. The west tower is the oldest part of what is now a mansion, which has changed from a Border stronghold, to what the old writers described as a 'gentleman's residence'. In a survey, carried out in 1542, the tower was 'in good reparations'. The drive from the main road is lined with trees which grow to great heights in this part of Northumberland. Close to the river, this house today has a most attractive setting.

Little Harle is not to be confused with Kirkharle Tower, which was already demolished when Tomlinson wrote his famous 'Guide' in 1891. It was the home of the Loraines, and only a small part of the tower escaped the demolition, and now forms part of a farmhouse. This picturesque part of the county is so rich in scenery and history, that it is impossible to do justice to the many places of interest within the pages of a book. Like many estates, Little Harle has had many different owners; firstly the de Harles, from whom the name was probably taken. In 1552, a John de Fenwick is mentioned as living in the tower; it then passed into the hands of the Aynsleys of Shaftoe, whose virtues are commemorated in Kirkwhelpington Church. The estate was then transferred by marriage, to Lord Charles Murray, the son of a Duke of Athol who assumed the name of Aynsley. How long this family remained the owners, it has not been possible to ascertain, but in 1851, the principal resident, to use a Victorian term, was Thomas Anderson.

A stranger exploring this district, where so many of the hamlets and villages have names strongly resembling each other, should be armed with an ordnance map, otherwise confusion can arise. Kirkheaton perhaps is the most difficult to find; there are no roads out! This is a typical Northumbrianism, and defies explanation. Certainly there are many ways by which the village can be approached, and it would appear logical if the same route were used for the return journey. Either from the Military Road, using many of the by-ways which intersect this part of Northumberland, and where there is very little traffic to be encountered, or from the Jedburgh road, near Belsay, the visitor to Kirkheaton can take his choice. It is also possible to use the road which branches off from Watling Street at the Five Lane Ends, and this is perhaps the most attractive way, as there are extensive views of the countryside from this road, which in its winding journey joins the main road near Kirkharle.

Kirkheaton was once part of the parish of Stamfordham, and in the nineteenth century it was described as an 'extra-parochial chapelry'. Completely rural now, in 1851 there was a colliery worked by William Grace & Co., while limekilns also provided work for the people of the district. At that time Kirkheaton was the property of the Bewick family. As the village is built on what the Victorians delighted in describing as an 'eminence', there are more delightful views, though the present writer, who has visited Kirkheaton on many occasions, is doubtful of the veracity of the Victorian writer who enthused over the views of the German Ocean and Gateshead Fell. This writer must have used imagination as well as binoculars!

The 'big' house is what was once one of the many fortified dwellings of Northumberland, and part of the tower still remains, and is incorporated in the present building. At one time this house, sometimes referred to as a manor house, was the vicarage. It is one of the many places where Cromwell is reputed to have stayed during his incursions into Northumberland. The church, which is dedicated to St Bartholmew, was built in 1775 at the expense of a Mrs D. Windsor, who was at that time Lady of the Manor.

Kirkheaton, unlike many Northumbrian villages is built round a village green, and many of the cottages have been restored and are used as weekend retreats. The writer has no intention of becoming involved in the controversial subject of 'foreigners' coming from the towns and using these cottages only in the summer months. Some of the 'foreigners' identify themselves with the village life and are an asset to the community, while others remain aloof and are never accepted by the local people.

It is one of the problems of country life in the 1960s, not only in the north, but in every rural community, that as fewer men are employed on the land, more houses and cottages are in danger of falling into decay, and ultimately becoming condemned property, were they not occupied by strangers. It is a subject which has to be approached from many different angles. The countryman is slow to make advances towards an 'in-comer' but the kindness of the Northumbrian, when the barriers have been bridged, is proverbial.

If the visitor has been able to find a way out of Kirkheaton, the journey to Capheaton, the most romantic village of them all, is the last but by no means the least interesting on this tour of the 'Kirks' and 'Heatons' of Northumberland. The Hall and the village are approached from the north by a road leading from the A696 which delights in the name of Silver Lane. In the year of the Forty-five Rebellion, some workmen discovered not only Roman coins but silver dishes and vessels dating from the days of the Roman occupation. These men, realizing that they had unearthed something of value, instead of handing over the treasures to their master, sold some of the silver, after they had broken it up, and disposed of all the coins. Fearing that someone might become aware of their dishonesty, they handed over the rest of the silver which they had not yet sold.

History does not record whether, or not, Sir John Swinburne was suspicious, and if any action was taken against his shifty employees. Surely suspicions must have been roused, when a silversmith in Newcastle recognized the stolen property, and handed it over to the owner of Capheaton. At a later date, some of the treasure found in Silver Lane was given to the British Museum by a nineteenth-century Swinburne.

As long ago as the sixteenth century Leland quoted a report by a contemporary Somerset Herald, that he had visited "A faire castle, in the midste of Northumberland, as in the bredthe of it. It was a IIII or V miles from fenwicke pile, and is the oldist house of the Swinburnes." This long forgotten castle was referred to as Hutton, and had a beacon on its tower, by which warning could be given to neighbours of approaching enemies. This 'pile', as Leland terms it, was bought by the Swinburnes from the Fenwicks in 1247. Until 1695 this family also possessed the castle in North Tynedale which bears their name.

The Swinburnes have always been a prominent family in the County, and today there are descendants of the family living in the beautiful Hall which was designed by Trollop. The son of Major and Mrs Browne-Swinburne now occupies part of the Hall, which for many years was empty.

Supporters of the House of Stuart, this ancient family was involved in the Civil War, and even more so in the Jacobite Rebellions, especially that of the 'Fifteen'.

A baronetcy was conferred on a John Swinburne by Charles I, but this patent was never taken out, not surprisingly, as he was the unfortunate young man who was murdered by Colonel Salkeld of Rock, at Meldon 'Gaits'.

There is a most romantic story concerning his son John, who was ultimately the first Swinburne to be elevated to a baronetcy. But before this happened, the heir to the Swinburne estates was missing for many years. After being sent to France for safety from the Parliamentarians, the boy became lost. A member of the

Radcliffe family, which was the name of the unfortunate Earls of Derwentwater and to whom the Swinburnes were related, was in France, and quite by chance, visited a monastery, where he noticed a boy who bore a strong resemblance to his Swinburne relatives. On being questioned, the boy said that he had always understood that his name was John Swinburne. His memories of his childhood in Northumberland were so clear, that after much interrogation, he was accepted as the son of John Swinburne, who had married Ann Blount. Such was the accuracy of the future baronet's memory, that he even described the markings of a cat at Capheaton.

This Sir John married Isabell, daughter of Henry Lawson of Brough in Yorkshire, and they became the parents of twenty-four children, of whom thirteen were daughters. It is not surprising that this family needed a larger house; and so in 1688 the present Hall became their home.

The word '*sylvan*' does not usually appeal to the writer, though it seems the most appropriate adjective to apply to Capheaton Hall, which is set in such delightful and sheltered surroundings, with its lake and avenue of tall trees. It is a house which should be better known, as with its architecture and wealth of history, it is one of the most fascinating of Northumberland's many 'big' houses.

The estate is well run and managed, the cottages in the village have well kept gardens. Altogether Capheaton is a joy to visit. It requires the pen of Algernon Charles Swinburne to describe the beauties of this home of his ancestors in some of his verse:

> Between our eastward and our westward sea
> The narrowing strand
> Clasps close the noblest shore fame holds in fee
> Even here where English birth sets all men free—
> Northumberland.
> The splendour and the strength of storm and fight
> Sustain the song
> That filled our father's hearts with joy to smite
> To live, to love, to lay down life that right
> Might tread down wrong.

They warred, they sang, they triumphed, and they passed,
And left us glad
Here to be born their sons, whose hearts hold fast
The proud old love no change can overcast,
No chance leave sad.

10

The Countess of Darwentwater

Oh, could the human hand obtain
Then all it would bestow,
Again would Countess Amelia reign
Where her sires did long ago.
Then justice, mercy, and gratitude,
Go hand in hand,
And give to the heart its latitude,
And Countess Amelia her land.

THIS unfortunate attempt to break into verse is the work of a Professor Softley of Corbridge, and are "Lines dedicated to Amelia, Countess & Heiress of Darwentwater, on the morning her Ladyship entered Dilstone [*sic*] Castle, the ruined abode of her Grandfather, 29th September, 1868".

Who was this extraordinary woman, the cause of such commotion and drama in South Tynedale in the late '60s and early '70s of the last century? Styling herself 'Lady Amelia Mary Tudor Radcliffe' and subsequently, 'Amelia, Countess of Darwentwater', she claimed direct descent from James, third Earl of Derwentwater, and was entitled to the vast estates of her 'ancestors'. After the execution of the third Earl in 1716, the estates were sequestrated and were administered by the Crown and ultimately by the Greenwich Hospital Commissioners. Their most popular agent was John Grey of Milfield near Wooler, the father of Josephine Butler, the social reformer. John Grey was succeeded as agent by his son Charles who was involved in the affairs of Amelia.

The facts accepted by history are that the only son of the third Earl died in 1731 at the early age of 27 and is buried beside his mother at Louvain. Therefore there was no direct male descendant of "Derwentwater's bonnie martyred Earl", his only other child, a daughter, having married Lord Petre.

Amelia's story (which often varied) was that the titular Earl had not died in 1731, that the facts had been concealed by the Government, and that he, John, had married one Elizabeth Arabella Maria Countess Waldsteine Waters in 1740, and by her had two children, one of whom, John James, was the father of Amelia, her mother being Amelia Anna Charlotte, Princess Sobieska. The other child of this marriage was, according to the Lady Amelia, her brother, the last titular Earl of Derwentwater, who died unmarried in 1854, leaving the field clear for Amelia Mary Tudor Radcliffe.

The complications of the sequestrated estates, and the collateral Radcliffes have been most ably dealt with by Ralph Arnold in his very informative book *Northern Lights*.

Claimants throughout history, whether genuine or bogus, have had an endless appeal and attracted supporters to their cause; Amelia was no exception. She had a loyal supporter for a time, in the Rector of Blaydon, the Reverend William Brown. This worthy gentleman's loyalty must have been somewhat strained when Amelia began borrowing money from him, although he was one of the few ever to be repaid.

The first appearance in the North of this leading lady in the 'Darwentwater' drama (this form of spelling Amelia always used) was at Blaydon in County Durham, where she lived in a small terrace house. There are no records but her own to tell us where she came from and these are open to speculation.

For some years Amelia had been writing letters (she was a prolific and fertile letter writer) to Lord Petre on the subject of her claim, even calling at his house in Essex. Having made no headway there, she apparently moved North, and became 'news' after an interview with the *Newcastle Weekly Chronicle* in 1866.

According to her supporters, this accomplished and fascinating lady must have been a journalist's dream; persecuted, misunderstood, fighting for her ancestral home, she was a front page story, and the leading lady knew how to exploit her publicity. The popularity of the Derwentwaters still lingered in Tynedale, and there were many attracted to the claimant's cause, possibly against their better judgment, but who still hoped to see Dilston once more the home of a Radcliffe.

Little remained of the glories that had once been Dilston, near Corbridge on the Tyne. The great house which the third Earl had built had been demolished, and the present Dilston Hall had not yet been built. All that remained of the original castle was the ruined Pele tower, and a wing known as the nursery wing, but there was money at stake, and this perhaps was the strongest motive in Amelia's fight for her 'rights'.

The writer, having discussed Amelia's claim with those who have intimate knowledge of the case, is convinced that she was an imposter, but who she really was can never be established.

It 1869 a book appeared entitled:

Jottings of Original Matter
From the Diary of
Amelia, Countess and Heiress
of Darwentwater
and from
The Journal of her Grandfather, John,
4th Earl of Darwentwater,
Devilstone Alias Dilstone Castle,

———————

Printed in London
and
Sold in Newcastle-on-Tyne, Blaydon, Corbridge, Hexham,
and at
Different Stations between Newcastle and Carlisle.
1869 (Copyright reserved)
By Lovers of Justice.

The *Jottings* make fascinating reading, but unfortunately little or no reliance can be placed on the contents, as under pressure Amelia admitted that she was the author.

At this time someone must have been supplying the enterprising writer with money, as the *Jottings* are beautifully bound in vellum, embossed with an earl's coronet, and include many sketches and a self portrait by the gifted authoress. Certainly Amelia had no inferiority complex, as extracts from the *Jottings* prove: "Lovers of Justice" tell us that "She can vie with the most industrious and talented ladies of her Majesty's realm. Her unusual attainments and the accuracy of her knowledge on all the subjects of which she converses are remarkable. She is always able to give her authorities—her memory is most wonderful. Her passion for the beauty of material nature is one of her marked characteristics. She expresses in her person all that is dignified, and artists look at her paintings with reverence, and call them masterpieces. . . . Her Ladyship has no jealous or unchristian feeling running through her unselfish breast; and we are happy to say that the Amelia, Countess of Darwentwater has no grievous blights of fashionable gambling, and was never on a race-course in her whole life . . . ." In fact, in her own estimation Amelia was a paragon of virtue. It would be interesting to know if any of the 'masterpieces' still exist.

According to Amelia, she was born at Dover in 1830, but she does not give any details of her birthplace. This leads one to believe that her origins were humble, which of course she would never divulge, as she later suffered from delusions of grandeur.

Orphaned at an early age, the future countess and her brother, the titular earl, spent their youth wandering about the Continent under the care of trustees. Amelia was a most precocious child, and the seeds of her future ambition appear to have taken root when she was about eight years old. Her godmother of course was Royal, the Land Gräffin of Hessen Homburg, who, Amelia relates, insisted that her talented godchild should be confirmed by the Archbishop of Canterbury. So Amelia conveniently switched from the faith of her forebears to that of the Established Church. Surely had this event taken place some records would be in existence. One thing is certain: had any awkward questions been asked, Amelia would have had her answer ready!

The family pedigree, which is given in full in *Jottings*, is, she explains, the only genuine record of the Radcliffe family: any others were supposition, as the originals had been concealed from the public by "the cruel enemies of the fallen family". Amelia was not going to be caught out if she could help it.

Many and varied are the wanderings of Amelia and her brother, or so she would have her readers believe; a visit to Longleat in Wiltshire inspired the budding artist to execute a sketch of the then Marquis of Bath falling off his donkey (this unusual sketch is including in *Jottings*), travels in Switzerland, painting lessons in Düsseldorf, a visit to Italy, and to several of the German States seem to have occupied most of their time. It was in Germany that this remarkable brother and sister lost their reputed fortune "owing to the unsettled state of that country". *Jottings* records that the so-called titular earl helped to effect the escape of Louis Philippe, King of France, to England, afterwards returning to France, where he witnessed the assassination of one of his mother's relations, the Princess Lichnousky, from which sorrow he never recovered. The young earl therefore made his will in favour of his sister; however, before his death in 1854, John Radcliffe (if that was really his name) visited the Lake District with his sister where she explored the Derwentwater estates.

It seems that it was after the death of her brother that Amelia seriously set about her campaign, and came to live at Blaydon. Where she lived in the interim and why she chose to live in Blaydon she does not explain.

It has been suggested that Amelia may have been a German, but her handwriting bears no evidence of the Continental style, as the photostat below shows. This is typical 'Victorian' script:

John Clayton was a Newcastle solicitor, whom the 'Countess' regarded as one of her most bitter enemies. It was he who acted on behalf of one Joseph Laycock, whose land at Whittonstall, on the Durham-Northumberland border, originally Greenwich Hospital property, Amelia regarded as hers. The father of Sir William Gibson had a great deal to do with the legal battle between Amelia and her opponents, and to quote Sir William's words,

"I have always thought that in some ways the methods of the Admiralty in dealing—or not dealing—with Amelia's claim were calculated to arouse suspicion. . . . but that Amelia was an imposter I have no doubt. I think she may have been a maid to some of the many titled ladies more or less involved and was fairly well educated and became an adventuress and had a strange career. . . . I am sure that my father would not have taken the small part that he did in the defeat of Amelia if he had not been well satisfied that she was an imposter. . . . It seems unlikely that the problem will ever be solved".

The writer wonders if Amelia could at one time have been on the stage? She had all the attributes of an actress, and undoubtedly a strong sense of the dramatic. It seems sad that the Derwentwater story, that of James Radcliffe of the 'Fifteen' should have such a squalid tail-piece. Not that a claimant to great estates was or is unique, especially when the direct lines have died out. In the nineteenth century, two old gentlemen in the Highlands called themselves the Sobieski Stuarts, and claimed to be descendants of Bonnie Prince Charlie, but in their case there were no estates to complicate the matter. The most famous claimant of modern times was no doubt the young man who was widely known as the Tichborne Claimant.

That Amelia had studied the Radcliffe history there is no denial, and that she also possessed many letters, documents, copies of wills and personal articles. Many of these may have been forgeries, and her remarkable paintings, copies. It would be easy at that time to buy furniture which had been in the possession of the Earls of Derwentwater. People would be eager to have mementoes of this greatly loved family. The writer remembers a four-poster bed in her grandfather's home, which was reputed to have come from

Dilston. Later, when Amelia was asked to produce original letters or other evidence to prove her case, she always affirmed that they had been sent to someone who had never returned them! The key to the family jewel box was alleged to be "concealed in the east end chapel at Lumley Castle, County Durham".

The overtures were now over, countless letters had been, and were still to be written on both sides of this dispute. The Derwentwater furniture, and the priceless art 'treasures' were in a furniture repository at Blaydon, and accompanied by two bodyguards, or as Amelia preferred to call them, "my squires", she set out from Blaydon for Dilston on 28th September, 1868. A strange sight it must have been, the 'Countess' arrayed in an Austrian Military cloak, sitting on a wagon driven by Mr Samuel Aiston, and guarded by her 'squires', one of whom was a porter at Blaydon station, and the other, Aiston's son, a keelman. For a lady with such ideas of grandeur one would have thought Amelia's 'squires' would have been drawn from higher ranks of society!

In the early hours of the 29th September, Amelia took over the ruins of her ancestral home. In the *Jottings* there is a pathetic self portrait of this nineteenth-century squatter sitting under a tarpaulin awning, wearing the military cloak, and a feathered hat, calmly writing one of the many letters with which she inundated her fictitious grand friends. By this time the news had reached Charles Grey and he was mustering his forces.

Amelia could not have chosen a more romantic or pathetic setting for her exploit: the ruined tower, the neglected chapel where many Radcliffes had found their last resting place, and the murmur of the Devilswater in the ravine below. Today Dilston has a sad and neglected feeling, and in September of 1868 it was the perfect background for a persecuted heiress; the crumbling winding stair, the roofless room, where the 'squires' were busy hanging pictures on the bare walls when Charles Grey arrived, the man whom Amelia referred to as "the dingy grey man". What followed is pure melodrama: Amelia refused to listen to Charles Grey, asserting that she would rather die than leave her castle, whereupon the Agent for Greenwich Hospital beat a retreat to fetch help, returning with a colleague, a Mr Fenwick of

Newcastle. Supporters were gathering outside; Amelia's 'squires' were dressed in armour (for what reason is never explained). As force seemed the only solution, Charles Grey ordered his henchmen to remove Amelia by lifting her chair from which she had refused to move. It must have been the most extraordinary scene; by this time the enraged countess was brandishing a sword which she had brought with her (she seems to have been very military minded). Mercifully this dangerous weapon was seized from her before any damage was done, and the Countess of Darwentwater was removed from her home in a most undignified manner. Dumping her on the road outside the gates of Dilston, the distracted Mr Grey offered to transport her to whatever destination she wished to go. Amelia declined, and very soon her 'squires' had rigged up a tent for her, which became a gathering point for supporters, local residents, and curious sightseers from near and far. It was not every day that a countess could be seen sitting in a ditch. No wonder that Amelia died at the early age of forty-nine; these privations which she inflicted upon herself must have done her constitution irreparable harm.

When she refused to leave her tent, a small wooden hut was brought from Blaydon, and the now miserable, cold and unhappy woman remained there for some time until the Hexham magistrates took action. Amelia removed herself to Haydon Bridge, about nine miles to the west of Dilston, on the Newcastle–Carlisle road, where she took a room at the Anchor Inn, a coaching house which still dispenses hospitality. In its long existence the Anchor can never have had a stranger or more colourful visitor than Amelia.

The Anchor did not entertain its distinguished visitor for long, as Charles Grey arrived on the scene to collect Greenwich Hospital rents. After a few days the intrepid Amelia returned to the Inn, only to be forcibly ejected, but not before she brandished a sword (of which she seems to have had several, as she even bequeathed one in her will).

From now until 1874, the 'goings on' of Amelia kept the Greenwich Hospital Commissioners in a turmoil. Support for the 'heiress' ebbed and flowed, and eventually she lost the sympathy of the press. One of the most dramatic incidents occurred at the

Wylam as it once was
The birthplace of George Stephenson

farm of Newlands, near Whittonstall. Amelia, once again claiming possession, ordered a sale of the farm stock, which actually took place in scenes that can only be described as riotous. The police were called in to restore order, while Amelia's supporters cheered; more than two thousand people were involved in this fracas. The Chief Constable of Northumberland, General Allgood, regarded the situation as so serious that he himself was present in his official capacity. Prior to this demonstration, some of the Newlands stock had been sold at Consett, and Amelia pocketed the sum of £140.

The following years, until eventually she gave up the battle, could be described as the years of litigation. Summonses were issued, copies of which are still in existence, and the case came up at the Assizes in Newcastle in 1870. Amelia was accused of trespassing on the Greenwich Hospital estates, and the Commissioners were awarded damages amounting to £500. Already the indefatigable 'Countess' had addressed two petitions to Queen Victoria whom she describes as 'gentle', hardly a suitable adjective to apply to the Queen! The Prime Minister, Mr Gladstone, was her next target of appeal; he must have been somewhat surprised after reading the imposing letter heading 'Dilston Domain Estate Office' complete with an Earl's coronet, to see that replies were to be sent c/o Shotley Bridge Post Office! Amelia's world was composed of the sublime and the ridiculous.

The creditors were now pressing for their money, and a sale of the 'treasures', which was stopped after the amount owing had been realized, took place in Newcastle. It would be too long and involved to go into the many vicissitudes which befell this comic and at the same time pathetic woman who seemed to have travelled at this time in her amazing career between London and Shotley Bridge. It would be interesting to know who supplied her with money, and incited her to yet more ridiculous actions. Backers she must have had, as she had already been accused of contempt of court, and was eventually adjudged a bankrupt. According to one local legend Amelia took refuge in a house in Hencotes in Hexham, and that she used to lower a basket from an upper window into which her supporters placed food.

I

Wallington of 'Shew me the Way'

At last all the famous works of art and the Derwentwater relics came under the hammer, and brought miserably small prices for such masterpieces, pictures reputed to be by Kneller and Rubens being sold for £4 15s. and £4 10s. Some people must have picked up bargains!

Time after time the battling Countess ignored summonses to appear in court, and eventually was imprisoned in Newcastle, naturally staging one of her famous scenes when she was released, and having to be carried out of her cell. The rest of this extraordinary woman's life was spent in obscurity in the Consett district which seems to have held a peculiar attraction for her. Her last home was one room in Cutler's Hall Road, Benfieldside. This may have been coincidence that she found peace amongst the Germans who gave their name to this road, and who, by their skill in the steel trade could be said to be the forerunners of the Consett Iron Company! Had she any German connections, as some writers have suggested? The tantalizing suppositions are legion.

The only tangible reminders left of this stormy period in the history of Corbridge and the adjoining district are bundles of legal documents, yellowed with time, and tied up with frayed pink tape. One of her original letters to John Clayton of Chesters is in this collection, four closely written pages which read as follows:

To John Clayton Esqr.
Solicitor
Newcastle on Tyne.
30th Dec^{ber} 1874.

Sir
I am in receipt of your Note sent to My Bailiff Mr Brown to be forwarded to Me.

I have made him acquainted with My objections to the Bonds the s^d John Hare did not bring his replevin Action within the Time proposed by My Tenant Mr John Hare Farmer—whom you are defending in a replevin Action.

I have also written to the Registrar informing him of the Fact that allowed by the Law 5 clear Days: and therefore his Replevy is not tenable—and it would have been more practicable on your Part if you had told Hare the Law—as he did not only maltreat the Bailiffs by beating them and threatning to shoot the Men but he assailled the Dignity of Her Majesty's Law: it received a blow as well as the Man Hare told them—there was no Law he cared for.

I may mention the asparity you have expressed in your Note to My Bailiff for Me is cowardly and unmanly—but it betrays how much the Title of My Patriot Grandsires stabs—your self interest at Heart. It reflects the highest Light on My entailed Darwentwater Land which you have by dishonourable Means believed you had secured to yourself and thus you have presumed to Step farther and interfered with My Birth-Right—Is it manly of you to do so? Your superior Judges will inform you that the Law of England holds everything a Libel that is spaken in malice to injure a Person's Character in Society.

I here remind You when you bite John 6th Earl of Darwentwater's Child you bite a File that can file your conveyance to the level of your own unworthy Actions on the entailed Darwentwater Land: by which you have made yourself such a splendid existence and advised your clients to enter into similar transactions which you know to be contrary to the Statute and constitutional Laws of England to interfere in any way with entailed family Property.

With what countenance dare you appear on our entailed Darwentwater Land branded as you are with this notorious breach of Trust in your Profession as an Attorney.

I thank you for giving Me this fair opportunity of asking you from Whom did you obtain permission to enter upon My entailed Darwentwater Land. Not from Her Majesty the Queen either in Her Political or private Capacity—And not from the House of Lords. No, neither the Queen nor the House of Lords are the Owners of the entailed Darwentwater Land—The Queen is the Trustee of the entailed Darwentwater Estates—but She cannot allienate and cannot "Waste". The legal Estate or entail is in the Heir's of the Body of the elder Lineage for ever and they cannot allienate one Inch from that comprised in certain family Deeds of Settlement.

But the query is by what means you have been allowed to stalk over our entailed Lands? England has been a cruel Mother to Darwentwater's Children to allow Persons like yourself to rob and feast on Darwentwater Rights—And for your pecunary views you are obliged to hate and insult us. I resent your base insult becoming a Lady of Honour.

The Countess of Darwentwater
& Baroness of Langley.

The original spelling confirms the impression that Amelia was illiterate. Let this letter be Amelia's own epitaph; convinced that she was a great lady until the end, she requested that she should be buried beside her 'ancestors' in St Mary's Roman Catholic Church graveyard at Hexham. This request was not granted when she died in 1880. "Amelia, Countess of Darwentwater, Baroness Langley", was laid to rest in Blackhill Cemetery.

11

Old Histories and Historians of The County

O wad some Power the giftie gie us,
To see oursels as ithers see us!
It wad frae mony a blunder free us,
An' foolish notion.

—Burns

MANY and varied are the histories of Northumberland which have been written in the past. It is most illuminating to read today what these old historians thought of this vast county.

Certainly the earlier historians had no inhibitions, and delighted in expressing their own opinions, complimentary or otherwise. In fact it is difficult to reconcile some of the descriptions of places which are now regarded as beauty spots, with the dreadful pictures some of these candid writers convey.

Camden, who visited the Roman Wall, in his *Britannia* written in 1587, said he was afraid to cross the border from Cumberland into Northumberland, and gives the reason; "From thence it goeth forward to Busy Gap, a place infamous for thieving and robbery, but I could not with safety take the full survey of it for rank robbers there about". The Northumbrians had certainly built up a terrible reputation for themselves by their lawless way of living.

Leland, who was also a visitor in the sixteenth century, made varying reports; Morpeth impressed him as being a pleasant town, but for Alnwick he had little praise.

Naturally the Roman Wall has always been a great source of interest to historians, and in 1863, Dr J. Collingwood Bruce F.S.A., wrote his *Handbook To The Roman Wall*, which is now

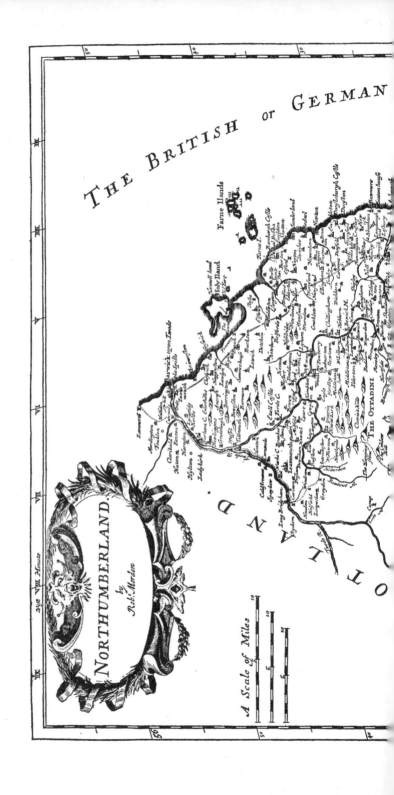

THE BRITISH or GERMAN

NORTHUMBERLAND.
by
Rob.ʳ Morden

A Scale of Miles

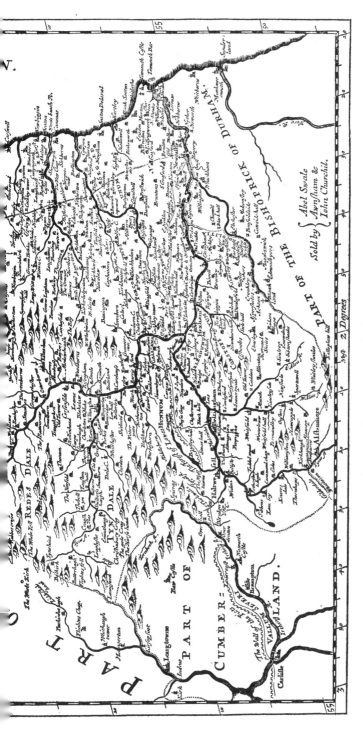

From a map of 1695

regarded as standard. Running into seven editions, its original title was *The Wallet Book of the Roman Wall*, and remained so until 1884. During the last twenty years, a shortened edition has appeared, revised and brought up to date by the late Professor Ian Richmond, of Newcastle, and subsequently of Oxford.

Collingwood Bruce, in the preface to the second edition, describes Hadrian's Wall: "The grandest monument of the daring, the power, and the determination of the Romans which is to be found in the dominions of our most gracious Sovereign Lady, Victoria—dominions on which the sun never sets—is to be found in the Northern Counties of England. Educated Englishmen cannot but wish to visit the Wall of Hadrian which stretches from the estuary of the Tyne to the waters of the Solway Firth. To assist them in doing so this Handbook has been prepared".

Unhappily the description of Queen Victoria's dominions is not appropriate today, and no doubt this loyal subject of his Sovereign Lady would be sadly distressed, were he living now, to see the sun setting on what was once a mighty Empire.

Long before the time of Collingwood Bruce, a Northumbrian, John Horsley by name, wrote his *Britannia Romana*, or *Roman Antiquities of Britain*, which brought him national fame. It is perhaps more accurate to describe this brilliant man as an antiquary, rather than an historian and it is as such that his name is inscribed on a plaque in Newcastle Royal Grammar School, of which he was a pupil. This John Horsley must not be confused with Thomas Horsley, a merchant, who, at his death in about 1545, left part of his fortune to found the school. The merchant Horsley was five time Mayor of the City of Newcastle, and it is he whose name occurs in the School song. The birthplace in 1685 of the later Horsley is not known but it is thought that it was either in or near Newcastle.

After completing his education at the Royal Grammar School, as the school is familiarly known today, John Horsley became a student at Edinburgh University, where he gained an Arts degree. Later taking Holy Orders, his first living was at Morpeth in his native county.

Like many writers, John Horsley's life was short; he was only forty-six when he died in 1731. His most outstanding work was *Romana Britannia* in three volumes which he illustrated with about a hundred copperplates. Remarkable as this gigantic task was, it is difficult to believe that according to a Victorian biographer of John Horsley, he "started upon his self-imposed task with no guide or handbook to the subject!" Surely even a man with an exceptional brain such as his, must have consulted earlier authorities. It is tragic, that owing to his early death, he did not live to see his work published.

A second historian in Holy Orders was the nineteenth-century parson, the Rev. John Hodgson, who wrote the first volumes of the County History.

As a change from clerical historians, a school-master, Eneas Mackenzie, was responsible for a history of Northumberland in two volumes, which first made its appearance in the early nineteenth century. Ironically this writer was a Scotsman born in Aberdeen in 1777, who came to live in Newcastle when he was only three years old; so he could be described as a Northumbrian by adoption. Mackenzie spent the rest of his life in his adopted city and presided over a school in High Bridge. He was also responsible for the founding of the Mechanic's Institute, but it is as a historian that he is remembered. He died at the age of fifty-five in 1832.

The amount of detail in Mackenzie's two large volumes is almost incredible. The history and scenery of the county is approached from every possible aspect: "Comprehending the various subjects of Natural, Civil and Ecclesiastical Geography, Agriculture, Mines, Manufactures, Trade, Commerce, Buildings, Antiquities, Curiosities, Public Institutions, Population, Customs, Biography, Local History etc. etc." Mr Mackenzie must have been a dauntless man to set himself so colossal an undertaking. How did he manage to look after his school as well?

Not content with 'presenting' his study of Northumberland and Northumbrians to the public (the closely printed volumes run to nearly five hundred pages on quarto-sized paper), he was also the author of *The History of Egypt* and editor of *Modern*

Geography, Select Biography, Life of Napoleon Bonaparte, etc. Eneas
certainly had a wide variety of interests and was prepared to go
into print on a great number of them. A second edition of *An
Historical, Topographical and Descriptive View of the County of Northumberland and of those parts of The County of Durham Situated North
of the River Tyne, with Berwick upon Tweed, and brief notices of celebrated Places on The Scottish Border*, came out in 1825. According
to the preface, as the first edition had for some years been out of
print, the demand for a second one "became frequent and urgent".

The present writer is tempted to apply some of the remarks
in the preface to her own works; in it we are told in flowery
language that the editor apologizes for occasional inaccuracies,
particularly those arising from the distraction occasioned by
other necessary pursuits!

Nevertheless, in spite of acknowledged inaccuracies, this is
one of the most comprehensive histories of the county which
has ever been written and it is specially interesting as Mackenzie
was not a Northumbrian and therefore wrote without the pre-
judices of the native-born.

The style is somewhat laborious, and it is certainly not a bed-
side book, but for wealth of detail it has been—and will be—
essential reading for any subsequent historian of Northumberland.

There is little or no light relief; Eneas does not appear to have
had any sense of humour whatsoever. Parish by parish, ward by
ward, the reader is told in rather prosy language, but with the
utmost exactitude, the character of the people referred to in the
first chapter as aborigines. What their way of life was like, the
number of live stock on the farms and the acreages, the worth of
the various clergy's livings, and their patrons; in fact some of it
reads rather like a present-day White Paper.

Probably the Castle Ward West Division has changed more
than any other since Mackenzie's day; in this ward the population
has increased so much, particularly at Heddon-on-the-Wall,
Newburn, Walbottle, Throckley, Woolsington and Ponteland,
and several hamlets all of which Mackenzie would find difficulty in
recognizing today.

Heddon-on-the-Wall is described as a poor village ... there

was only one farm house, two public houses and some cottages for mechanics and labourers. The living of the Vicar was worth £35 and was the gift of the Crown. The vicarage, which is still standing, receives some praise from Mackenzie and so does the ancient church which stands in a prominent position above the village. Situated, as Heddon is, at the junction of the Military Road and the West or Low Road to Carlisle, there is now an endless stream of traffic passing through the village. Several new estates have been built and, as is to be expected, many of the streets and roads have Roman names.

It is as difficult to picture Heddon today as a 'poor' village, as it is to recognize the glowing description of early nineteenth-century Newburn. In 1811, when this description was written, Newburn was according to the writer situated in a delightful position on the banks of the Tyne. The houses, though old, were built on uneven ground and were most attractive, each house having a garden which added to the charms of the village. There had been plans to re-design this Tyneside village, "combining the industrial with the picturesque", but these had been abandoned. Mention is made of some industry, such as a file factory owned by the Spencers, the same family which was connected in later years with Spencer's Steel-Works. Not surprisingly a pit is mentioned.

Walbottle is given very little space and is merely a "pleasant pit village". Throckley too is given much the same treatment. Now as a result of ribbon building, it is difficult to know where one of these villages ends and the other begins. Today from Heddon-on-the-Wall to the city boundary of Newcastle at Denton Burn there are houses all the way. One might even say that it is at Heddon that the country ends and the rest of the scenery on both sides of the Tyne is industrial. One of the greatest eyesores is the power station at Stella which includes both sides of the river, yet in this overcrowded area there still remain some green fields and pleasant houses. One such is Heddon Hall, which was once the home of another historian of Northumberland, C. J. Bates.

The greatest changes since Mackenzie's day in the West Division of the Castle Ward have been at Woolsington and Ponteland.

At Woolsington, there is now Newcastle Airport which was only recently modernized. Vast acres of runways have replaced agricultural land. There are numerous housing estates, some of which, to use that most objectionable description used by the estate agents, are of 'executive' type. In Mackenzie's book he speaks of the Mansion House "tastefully ornamented with fine plantations". He goes on to quote another writer, Hutchinson, who says, "The prospect over this part of the county is so extraordinary, that I cannot forbear pointing it out to future ramblers". What was extraordinary Hutchinson does not say; he does, however, say that "Ponteland is seated in the depth of the vale, shrouded with a pretty grove". Ponteland now is, together with the ever expanding estate of Darras Hall, a dormitory for nearby Newcastle. Together with the noise of the planes taking off and landing at the city airport, and the heavy traffic which goes through Ponteland on its way north and south on the busy highway, it can hardly be described as a peaceful place "in the vale".

In the statistical returns for 1815 the annual value of the property which made up this ward was £25,223. The comparison with today's value is left to the imagination.

Should the reader wish to know more about the County in bygone days, Mackenzie will have the answer. He gives a list of subscribers, from which he says many names are omitted, a roll of every Sheriff of the county up to the day of publication and the name of every member of Parliament for the county.

The numbers of live stock are given with land values, and even pages are devoted to the various denominations which had their respective places of worship in the county. The Prebyterians in Northumberland are described as Protestant Dissenters and Mackenzie even explains with which groups over the Border they were in Communion! With the respect due to a man who did so much to preserve the history of Northumberland, Mackenzie has to be taken in small doses. Years must have been spent on research, and in those days, when communication was difficult, it is a wonder that he was able to visit so many places and obtain so much information. It is a relief in many ways to say "Farewell and thank you" to this garrulous and verbose writer, indispensable though his views and descriptions of his adopted county are to modern historians. For that tribute must be given to one of the 'Auld Enemy', who spent his lifetime in what, in the past, had been enemy territory.

W. W. Tomlinson, who was a Yorkshireman born in Driffield in 1838; he died in Newcastle in 1916. His occupation was as a clerk in the employment of the old North Eastern Railway. He was an entirely different type of writer from Mackenzie. His *Comprehensive Guide to Northumberland* was published in 1891, and although it lives up to its title of 'comprehensive' it is much easier to read and the style is quite different from the works of Mackenzie. Tomlinson was outspoken and appears to have revelled in flowery descriptions, yet his work is as useful to the historian today as when it first appeared.

It is a guide book, and although so many changes have taken place within the seventy-seven years since it was written, the accuracy is unquestionable even if the reader sometimes disagrees with his rather prejudiced opinions and acid comments. Not only did Tomlinson produce this classic, he was also responsible for *Life in Northumberland during the Sixteenth Century*.

Certainly this Yorkshireman was under no illusions regarding the behaviour of the earlier Northumbrians and he gives graphic descriptions of the unruly conditions which existed there in the sixteenth century. The 'guide' begins with a short introduction, then proceeds to describe district by district throughout the county. It is complete with maps, though these are of little help today. One noticeable point is that so many railways lines which intersected Northumberland in Tomlinson's day have now disappeared.

Hills and their heights, crags, denes, loughs, lakes etc, are listed separately, and there is also a very useful list of pre-Reformation churches. The principal camps of the ancient Britons are also tabulated, together with some of the principal castles and Pele towers. Roman stations and camps, even ruined churches and chapels and the remains of monastic houses are all included.

It is interesting to read what the writer considered the most important hotels in the county, and how many of them remain.

An advertisement at the end of the guide is a picture of a be-whiskered gentleman wearing an 'Inverness' cape, accompanied by a lady, who is sheltering under an umbrella. This advertisement was that of Henry A. Murton & Co., a firm long established in Newcastle, which was bought by the Co-operative Wholesale Society some years ago. In 1891 a tourist's waterproof, overalls, overcoat and hat cover cost 31s. 6d., complete in small shoulder case or strap; more expensive waterproof protection for the tourists who braved Northumberland's variable climate cost as much as 50s.

The manor of Wylam on the Tyne, which in the writer's opinion has many attractions, is dismissed in *The Guide to Northumberland* as "a large uninteresting village chiefly composed of pit-men's dwellings". Certainly Wylam sprang up as a result of the many collieries which were working in the district at that time, but the rows of houses still occupied—such as those near the church—are well built and pleasant. Coal was mined in early times near Wylam and a paper written by Mr W. H. Waugh, says that there were minerals worked there in Roman times. Coal, iron and lead have all contributed to the existence of this village on the Tyne.

It was a branch of the Blackett family who developed the coal trade in this part of Northumberland and land and property in Wylam and the surrounding district are still in the possession of this family today. The present squire lives in one of Wylam's attractive stone-built houses.

The picture which Wylam presents today is so different from Tomlinson's abrupt dismissal of it as an uninteresting village, that it deserves a fuller description. It has been described recently as a 'compromise' between town and country. Only ten and a half miles from Newcastle it is a popular place for people who work in the City of Newcastle to make their homes. Although many of Wylam's inhabitants today have come from other parts of the country, there is still, happily, a hard core of inhabitants who are proud of the fact that they have been born and bred in what, in the words of a local song writer, is 'Canny Wylam on the Tyne'.

It is extraordinary that the *Comprehensive Guide to Northumberland* devotes so little space to the district where George Stephenson was born, particularly as W. W. Tomlinson spent all his working life with what is now called British Rail.

In Wylam church there is a tablet bearing the following inscription:

> This church was built and endowed to the glory of God and in affectionate remembrance of the late William Hedley of Wylam, and Frances his wife, by their sons William and George Hedley of Burnhopeside Hall, Lanchester in the County of Durham.
>
> To the inventive genius of William Hedley at Wylam in 1812, and assisted by the perseverance of the late Christopher Blackett, Esqr., (at whose expense the experiments were made) the world is indebted for the first successful Locomotive Steam Engine.
>
> The building was commenced by George Hedley, who died shortly before its completion, and it was subsequently completed and endowed by his brother William. Anno Domini 1887.

The foundation stone was laid in 1885 by Mrs Richard Clayton and is dedicated to St Oswin. The first baby to be baptized in the new church was Mr Oswin Wilkinson, who is now 81 years of age and still lives in Wylam. The lych-gate was the gift of Richard Clayton, and within the church there is a brass plaque to the memory of Musgrave Ridley.

Blacketts, Ridleys and Claytons have all lived either at The Hall or Wylam Cottage, which are Wylam's two 'big' houses.

As Tomlinson's Guide was published in 1891, and the building of the church was completed in 1887, it is all the more curious that this usually meticulous historian makes no reference whatsoever to the changes taking place in Wylam. Perhaps he had completed the particular chapter in which he described 'Newcastle to Ovingham' and felt that he could not face revision!

To those who are unfamiliar with the district, Wylam is a confusing village. It is in two separate divisions, North and South Wylam, connected by a bridge over the Tyne; and to puzzle the stranger even more, there is a West Wylam on the south bank of the river, on the road which leads from Gateshead to Hexham.

The bridge over the river was a toll bridge until 1936, when, to quote from the plaque placed there by the County Council:

> This bridge was acquired by Northumberland County Council and freed from Tolls on 2nd December 1936.
>
> The piers were built in 1836 and supported a Colliery wagon way.
>
> Following extensive flood damage in 1957 the foundations were rebuilt. The superstructure was renewed and widened in 1960.

South Wylam is purely residential, many of the houses dating from the beginning of the century. Some stand on rising ground and have delightful views to the south into County Durham, which here is still rural. Close to Wylam station is the Boat House Inn, the only one on the south side of the river. There are records dating from 1795 when it was known as 'The Ferry Boat'. This building must have been in existence for some time before it became a public house as it is mentioned as having survived the great floods of 1771. These caused such havoc to the buildings and bridges of the Tyne Valley, that the bridge at Corbridge was the only one which withstood the force of the raging river.

A group of houses standing close to the bridge connecting the disused loop line from Newcastle to North Wylam with the main railway line to Carlisle is Hagg Bank. The word 'hagg', according to Heslop, means a fenced enclosure surrounded by trees, from which cattle were prohibited. Hodgson also says that the hays and haggs were grounds which were hedged round. The enclosure of trees at this strangely named hamlet bears out these theories.

North Wylam is built on ground which rises sharply from the Tyne by way of Holeyn Hall Road, to the busy West Turnpike. On the green near the bridge is the War Memorial, and nearby is a large modern building, used as a bakery by a grocery firm. This red brick building stands on the site of the flour mill, which was destroyed by fire in modern times. Some residents of the village can remember watching the flames in all their fury, and seeing the horrifying spectacle of hundreds of rats fleeing from the inferno. In gigantic letters the new building advertises itself as Wylam Mill.

Although there are new estates, and at the time of writing there is yet another in the process of erection, North Wylam has some delightful old houses which intermingle with the new. Outside 'Ye Olde Black Bull' is a stone mounting block, a reminder of the days when patrons of the Bull would ride long distances to quench their thirst. Wylam residents need never suffer from thirst as there are three other houses of call, 'The Ship' and 'The Fox and Hounds' and 'The Boathouse'.

At one time the villagers had the choice of two other houses of call where they could forgather for a pint. 'The Bird', and near the disused station of North Wylam the appropriately named 'Stephenson's Arms'.

The village is overlooked by the church the clock of which, chiming every quarter hour, is a constant reminder of the passing of time. There is also a typical Northumbrian farmhouse, in beautifully kept surroundings, marred only by the ugly silo towers which are a result of the changes in farming methods. Instead of 'winning' the hay as in days gone by, or even baling, as is so common today, the more modern method uses what is termed 'wilted' grass. This is stored and when preserved is fed as 'haylage' to dairy herds. The herd at Wylam Hills is Friesian, and although farming must keep pace with the times, it is regrettable that these all too obvious 'silos' cannot be made to blend more with the countryside.

As the land rises from the village there are the Old People's houses, built on land given by the present squire and so named 'Blackett Cottages'.

Wylam also has a recreation ground where bowls are played, and seats are provided for on-lookers.

There are so many organizations in Wylam, that if one joined them all there would be no time to do any work. Most of the meetings are held in the Institute, and at the beginning of November is held what is called 'Community Week' when various attractions are arranged to raise money to keep the Institute flourishing. Concerts, sports days and the anniversary of Guy Fawkes' unsuccessful plan to blow up The Houses of Parliament are celebrated. There is a fire-works display and a concert in which practically every organization in the village takes part.

K

What a very different village W. W. Tomlinson would see today, were he able to re-visit Wylam on the Tyne.

There is also another omission in this 'comprehensive' Guide which is remarkable. No mention is made of the viaduct at Kielder, designed by Peter Nicholson of Newcastle in 1840, at the head of the North Tyne, where the old North British Railway used to run. For a man employed by the railways this omission is a puzzle. It was said at the time that there was no one in the country who had the knowledge to design another! In 1967, a victory was won, for although the railway track between Hexham and the Scottish Border no longer exists, the viaduct, which, until the intervention of The Northumberland and Newcastle Society was under a threat of demolition, is now to remain. Thanks to the efforts of Sir Rupert Speir, for several years member of Parliament for the Hexham Division, and Colonel Richard Burn of Carrycoats Hall, money has been raised for the necessary repairs. £500 has been donated by the Sir James Knott Trust and another £500 was given by an anonymous donor. It is now up to the people of Northumberland to give generously to keep this memorial to the railway pioneers in a state of good repair.

It is extremely difficult for a writer to keep up with the times in these rapidly changing days, as, by the time the written word has gone to press, many landmarks have disappeared. At the time of writing this chapter, the Walls of Berwick upon Tweed are threatened with a breach, to make way for the ever increasing volume of traffic which passes through this ancient town— probably the most historic of all towns in the United Kingdom. Surely some plan can be evolved which will save these almost perfect Elizabethan walls from the incursion of modern times.

How much easier it must have been for the historians of the past, when there was time to look and linger, than it is in the present day when life is lived at such a tempo that there is hardly time to think.

Before this chapter is concluded thanks must be given to those men (why so very few women?) who have given their time and their energy to the study of the history of the County of Northumberland: Camden, Leland, Horsley, Mackenzie, Collingwood Bruce, Tomlinson, C. J. Bates, Howard Pease, Wallis, Sykes and Ian Richmond and a few women, Jessie Mothersole, Agnes Herbert and Jean Terry have all contributed to the history of this peerless County. It is salutary to see how others see us, as few of the historians of Northumberland have been Northumbrians by birth.

Now, in more enlightened days, we can take stock of ourselves, and have more tolerance for those who are not so conscious of their ancestry as are the Northumbrians.

12

Northumberland in Song and Verse

Where hev ye been aal the day,
Billy Boy, Billy Boy?
Where hev ye been aal the day me Billy Boy?

I've been walkin' aal the day,
With me charmin' Nancy Grey—
And me Nancy kittled me fancy,
Oh me charmin' Billy Boy.

—Northumbrian capstan shanty

NORTHUMBERLAND is rich in traditional songs and verse,
which can be divided roughly into three classes. The first are
sea shanties, which are sung the world over and require little or
no explanation; an example is 'Billy Boy', a verse from which is
quoted at the beginning of this chapter. Second are the songs and
tunes which are based on historical events and legends connected
with the county, the music of which was originally composed to
be played on the Northumbrian pipes. The third class could be
described as 'pitmatic', as many of the words in the Tyneside song
books depict events in the lives of workers in the coalfield.

The shanties were sung by the sailors while they heaved at the
capstan and windlass; all have a rousing chorus, and the tunes
were in rhythm with the efforts of the sailors as they 'heaved'.

Those who delight in the songs written in the days of the sailing ships, owe a debt of gratitude for their preservation to the
late Sir Richard Terry. Richard Runciman Terry was born in
Northumberland in 1865. He was the son of the village school-
master in the little village of Ellington, which is a short way in-

land from the coast, not far from the wide sweep of Druridge Bay. On his mother's side Richard Terry came of a seafaring family, which possibly accounted for his great love of songs and music connected with the sea especially those of his native county.

Honoured by his country in 1922 with a knighthood for his services to music, he was at one time musical director of Westminster Cathedral and composed five masses; in Northumberland he is remembered as the 'rescuer' of so many traditional songs, a collection of which was published in 1907. He died in 1938.

The many verses of 'Billy Boy' enumerate the qualities required in a sailor's wife. Nancy certainly had all the qualities required, "She can meak a feather bed fit for any sailor's head", but only a Northumbrian lass could have supplied Billy with the traditional cakes known as 'singing hinnies'. "She can meak an Irish stew, Aye and singin' hinnies too" says her sailor husband.

It may seem odd to include a recipe in a chapter on music and song, but in many traditional folk songs food is mentioned and certainly Billy Boy seems to have been extremely interested in Nancy's culinary arts! Singing hinnies are really a rich kind of girdle cake (Northumbrians always refer to the more usually termed griddle as a girdle, which can lead to complications unless this is explained). Compared with the amount of flour used in the making of these cakes the quantity of fat is excessive; this results in a hissing sound when the cakes are put on the hot girdle, hence the adjective 'singing'. Four ounces of butter is rubbed into a pound of flour, together with four ounces of lard. Two teaspoons of baking powder is added and a teaspoon of salt. The mixture is then rolled out and is put on the girdle in one piece and turned over and browned on both sides.

In some of the colliery districts this rich mixture is called by another name, 'Sma' coal fizzers' as so much small coal was used, and the fires in the pitmen's houses were never allowed to die out, as free coals were a perquisite of the miners.

Sir Richard did not confine his researches to Northumberland, and in *The Shanty Books* there are many which are international. *The Shanty Books* are in two parts, with a foreword by the then Sir Walter Runciman, Bt. who was a brother of the musician's mother. The Runciman family are ship-owners who founded the Moor Line, and lived at one time at Shoreston Hall near Seahouses and at Doxford which is now a home for old people.

The first Runciman baronetcy was created in 1906, on Walter, who was born not far from Ellington at Cresswell. In 1933, Sir Walter was raised to the peerage as Lord Runciman of Shoreston. His son, also a Walter, became a Viscount during the lifetime of his father and made politics his career. It was he who went to Czechoslovakia in the crisis of 1938 to make overtures to Hitler, which led to most unsatisfactory results; but the verdict of history is that the Führer never had any intention of coming to a peaceful arrangement.

The present Lord Runciman is the second Viscount of Doxford. From this family, who became so powerful in the world of shipping, have come musicians, writers and politicians. Sir Richard Terry's sister was the author of a most informative history of the county.

There are many other collections of the traditional songs by others, but for shanties, Sir Richard Terry's is the most widely known.

In *A Collection of Songs of Northern England*, collected and edited by John Stokoe is the story of 'The Bonny Fisher Lad'. Unfortunately no information is given about the origin, but the words suggest that this fisher laddie hailed from near Bamburgh; and as at one time, the nearby harbour of Seahouses was a busy fishing port, he may have sailed his coble from this rocky coast-line, which is dominated by the great castle of King Ida. It was Sir Walter Scott who immortalized this part of the Northumbrian coast in verse, but the writer of the simple folk song will for ever be anonymous.

> O the bonny fisher lad that brings fishes frae the sea.
> O the bonny fisher lad gat haud o' me.
> On Bamboroughshire's rocky shore,
> Just as you enter Boomer Raw
> There lives the bonny fisher lad,
> The fisher lad that bangs them a'.

These old song writers were not troubled about either spelling or geography, as in another verse Boomer becomes Bowmer!

As spelling only became standardized at the end of the eighteenth century, the variations are understandable.

Another ardent collector of the old songs who was a contemporary of Sir Richard Terry was W. G. Whittaker, one time music master at the old Rutherford Girls' School in Newcastle and who was also connected with Armstrong College as it was then known. Once part of the University of Durham, the name was changed to King's College, and has now been integrated into the University of Newcastle.

Born 1876, W. G. Whittaker published a collection not only of songs with a historical background, but also with those which have an industrial setting. Under the title of *North Country Songs Selected from North Countree Ballads, Songs and Pipe-Tunes* edited and arranged by W. G. Whittaker this is a most valuable collection.

Short histories of the tunes and songs are included, and in the case of the famous 'Elsie Marley' the tune was originally written for the Northumbrian pipes. Strictly speaking this folk song, which is often confused with a nursery rhyme, is set in County Durham, but as the Bishopric was at one time part of the kingdom of Northumbria it does not seem inappropriate to include it. Poor Elsie Marley who 'wouldn't get up to feed the swine' came to a sad end as she was drowned in 1768. Elsie's husband was landlord of 'The Barley Mow' at Pictree near Chester-le-Street, and a public house of the same name is still there. The ballad was written about incidents in Elsie's life, and was published by Joseph Ritson, in his *Bishopric Garland* of 1784.

Evidently this inn-keeper's wife developed ideas beyond her station in life, as not only would she not get up in the mornings, lying in bed 'till eight or nine', she also discarded her straw hat for a velvet bonnet, and the song goes on to say that "The Lambton lads mun pay for that, Di ye ken Elsie Marley honey?" The use of honey as a term of endearment here bears out the theory that the Northumbrian 'hinny' is a corruption of honey, or of anything that is sweet.

Naturally the most famous pipe tune is 'Chevy Chase', which is the traditional air played by the Duke of Northumberland's piper. Many times does the name of Percy occur in the ballad, the theme of which is to a great extent imaginary. It is doubtful if there ever was a battle of such a name; it is more likely to be the tale of several border forays merged into one to make a better story. There is no doubt that Otterburn was largely the basis of 'Chevy Chase' and there are several variations of the tune. The verses give vivid word pictures of the times and several are well worth quoting:

> God prosper long our noble king,
>   Our lives and safeties all!
> A woeful hunting once there did
>   In Chevy Chase befall.
>
> To drive the deer with hound and horn
>   Earl Percy took his way;
> The child may rue that is unborn
>   The hunting of that day.
>
> The stout Earl of Northumberland
>   A vow to God did make,
> His pleasure in the Scottish woods
>   Three summer's days to take.
>
> . . . These tidings to Earl Douglas came,
>   In Scotland where he lay . . .

Certainly the old ballad mongers cared little for geography, as Otterburn, which provides most of the material, is in Redesdale, while two of the other battles thought to be part of the fabric are Homildon Hill and Piperdean (or Piperden according to the spelling) which took place far away, one near Wooler, and the other about a mile from Mindrum. That Hotspur was present at two of these battles is certain, Otterburn and Homildon Hill. A Percy of those days was never far away if there was a chance of a good fight, especially if their deadly enemies the Douglases were involved. When the Douglas of the ballad heard that the Percys were hunting their deer he immediately set forth to meet them, and so the ballad goes on:

> At last these two stout Earls did meet,
>> Like captains of great might:
> Like lions wud, they laid on lead
>> And made a cruel fight.

The Douglas offered the Northumbrian Earl his life if he would surrender and pay ransom to the Scottish King. This offer Percy scornfully rejected,

> "No Douglas" quoth Lord Percy then,
>> "Thy proffer I do scorn;
> I will not yield to any Scot
>> That ever yet was born!"

Both Earls died fighting rather than yield to the other. In the days of 'Chevy Chase' life on the Borders was cheap;

> Of fifteen hundred Englishmen
>> Went home but fifty three,
> The rest were slain in Chevy Chase
>> Under the greenwood tree.

No wonder there is a tragic little poem 'The Border Widow's Lament'. In fact many of the Northumbrian folk songs are tinged with sadness, even if they are not connected with the battle-field that was Northumberland. A striking example is the plaintive 'Maa Bonny Lad', which was saved from oblivion by Sir Richard Terry.

There are only two verses extant;

> Hev ye seen owt o' maa bonny lad,
>> And are ye sure he's weel O?
> He's gyen ower land, wiv' his stick in his hand,
>> He's gyen to moor the keel O.

> Yes I've seen yor bonny lad,
>> Upon the sea I spied him,
> His grave is green, but not wi' grass,
>> And thou'll never lie aside him.

With its haunting melody 'Maa Bonny Lad' is one of the saddest of Northumbrian songs.

As a complete contrast is another song about a 'lad' but in this case although he went 'Doon the Wagon Way', which is the title of the song he did come home,

> Wiv his siller in his hand,
> An wi' love in his e'e,
> Yonder I see ma canny lad,
> A coming to me.

The beautiful river Coquet so famous for its fishing, has often been an inspiration for writers, and in 1825, two local song-writers, Robert Roxby and Thomas Doubleday jointly composed 'The Auld Fisher's Farewell to Coquet'. It appeared in a volume by the name of *The Fisher's Garlands*.

Again this song is nostalgic, as the old man who loved his river and his sport so dearly, laments the fact that he must 'gang again to Coquetside and take a farewell thraw'.

> Come bring to me my limber gad
> I've fished wi' mony a year,
> An' let me ha'e my weel worn creel,
> An' a' my fishing gear.
> The sunbeams glint on Linden Ha'
> The breeze comes frae the west,
> An' lovely looks the gowden morn
> On the streams that I love best.

This fisherman's lament as it could be termed, recalls the days of his youth, then as he grew older how his failing sight and the infirmities of old age made his last 'thraw' inevitable . . .

> An then fareweel, dear Coquet-side!
> Aye gaily may thou rin,
> An lead they waters sparkling on,
> An dash frae linn to linn;
> Blithe be the music of thy stream
> An banks through after-days,
> An blithe be every fisher's heart
> Shall ever tread they braes.

How delighted the nameless old man would be to know that Coquet is still a famous fishing river, and that the valley which he obviously loved so much is still largely unspoilt by the march of time.

Local families and their homes have also often been a theme of Northumbrian music; some of the pipe tunes, such as 'Blackett of Wylam' have no words, and this also applies to 'Fenwick of Bywell', the family which were once the owners of that enchanting hamlet on the Tyne.

Unfortunately little or nothing is known of the origin of the delightful 'Shew Me the Way to Wallington'. Advice which should be taken by many, as the 'way' leads to one of the county's most beautiful houses, which was at one time owned by the Fenwicks. The most dramatic approach is from the busy A696, as by this route 'The Way to Wallington' crosses the bridge which spans the Wansbeck. The words are so descriptive that the writer has no hesitation in quoting them in full.

O' Canny man, O! shew me the way to Wallington:
I've got a mare to ride, and she's a trick o' galloping;
I hae a lassie beside me, that winna give o'er her walloping,
O canny man, O! shew me the way to Wallington.

Weel or sorrow betide, I'll hae the way to Wallington,
I've a grey mare o' my ain, that n'er gives o'er her walloping;
I hae a lass forbye, that I cannot keep frae walloping;
O canny man, O! tell me the the way to Wallington.

Sandy, keep on the road, that's the way to Wallington,
Soon he reached Bingfield Kame, and by the banks O! Hallington;
Through Bavington Ha' and in ye go to Wallington;
Whether ye gallop or trot, ye'ere on the way to Wallington.

Off like the wind he went, clattering to Wallington;
Soon he reached Bingfield Kame, and passed the banks O'Hallington,
O'er by Bavington Syke the mare couldn't trot for galloping;
Now my dear lassie, I'll see, for I'm on my way to Wallington.

It is still possible to reach Wallington by following the directions given to the Sandy of the song, and when Wallington is reached, not only can the twentieth-century traveller see through the house and gardens, which are the property of the National Trust, but can have a meal at The Clock Tower, which provides refreshments for those who have found 'The Way to Wallington'.

On certain days the visitor to The Clock Tower can listen to the sweet sounding Northumbrian pipes played by Mrs Patricia Jennings and the Duke's piper, Mr Jack Armstrong. In fact by request the visitor may listen to 'Shew me the Way to Wallington' on its home ground.

Some of the songs are based on local customs as in the case of 'The Royal Earsdon Sword Dancers' Song'. These dancers have been famous for generations and a group of them still carry on the traditional custom and give displays. At one time these dancers from this village, which is situated in the industrial area of Northumberland not far from the sea, used to travel the county, giving displays at Alnwick Castle and other great castles and famous houses. They wear traditional costumes, and as long ago as 1829 a visit they made to Alnwick is mentioned. The dancers ask "good people to give ear to their story", which somewhat abbreviated is this;

> Five lads I've brought blithe and merry,
> Intending to give you a dance.
> Earsdon is our habitation,
> The place we were all born and bred;
> There are not finer lads in the nation,
> And none shall be gallanter led.

There are six more verses, all somewhat repetitive, and certainly the Earsdon sword dancers had no hesitation about self-advertisement, as the last verse proclaims them as 'five noble heroes' . . .

> And each bear as good a character
> As any five heroes on earth.
> If they be as good as their fathers,
> Their deeds are deserving records;
> It is all the whole company desires,
> To see how they handle their swords.

Two lines at the beginning of the fifth verse are somewhat

peculiar, as they proclaim that one of the dancers in this Northumbrian village was the son of "Lord Nelson, He that fought at the Nile". Perhaps it is wiser not to make any investigations regarding this statement.

It is quite impossible in a chapter such as this, to place on record a complete list of all who have helped to preserve the songs and music of their native county; nor is it possible to include the titles and origins of many well-known songs and poems.

Tribute, however, must be paid to a man who in a different way has made some of these songs familiar to so many people far away from his own county, and that man is Owen Brannigan, whose name needs no introduction to any lover of music. Born in 1908 at the colliery village of Annitsford, Owen Brannigan has gained international fame as a bass singer. A list of his successes is staggering and takes up a great deal of *Who's Who*. Glyndebourne, Covent Garden, Sadler's Wells Opera, the Paris Opera House, and most of the musical centres abroad have heard his magnificent voice. Not only does Owen Brannigan sing the songs of his own county, he is an opera singer of world renown.

In 1958 the Pope honoured this boy who sang in the choir of the Roman Catholic Church at Annitsford, by conferring on him the Papal Cross. Another honour came in 1964 when Queen Elizabeth decorated him with an O.B.E. Despite his fame, Owen Brannigan has not forgotten his North Country origin, and has several times returned and sung at events to raise money for causes in which he is interested. Recently Northumbrians had the opportunity of hearing him at Matfen Hall, where a concert was given to raise money for the Cheshire Homes, of which Matfen is the latest addition. For a Northumbrian it is an unforgettable experience to hear his glorious voice singing the familiar songs, of which 'Water of Tyne' is perhaps the most beautiful. Owen Brannigan does not forget the characteristic Tyneside songs in his repertoire, and there is usually a request for the Tyneside 'National Anthem' 'Blaydon Races'.

The pitmen's songs are of an entirely different type from the old Northumbrian melodies. Many of them were written in the last century by miners, and, as opposed to the somewhat sad themes of former days are often comical, dealing with events in the family, the 'gannin's on' of the neighbours and the cleverness of domestic animals, especially dogs. At one time a pitman when 'off shift' was rarely seen without a whippet at his heels.

Joe Wilson became famous for this type of song, and a review of his *Tyneside Songs and Drolleries* which appeared in *The Newcastle Journal* says "There are songs and pieces which possess not only the broad native humour, suited to the native dialect, but which are entitled to be ranked as true lyric poetry; Joe Wilson was gifted to write real songs for Tyneside people; they are racy and of the soil, and are a store house of the broad Doric of the district". It is sad to relate that this gifted man died when he was only thirty-four, but as long as his songs are sung he will be remembered. 'Geordie, Haud the Bairn' is one of Joe Wilson's most famous, and is so typical of the people of Tyneside in the last century. Those who are unable to understand the language can always refer to the chapter on speech in the early part of this book!

> Cum, Geordy, haud the bairn,
>   Aw's sure aw'll not stop lang;
> Aw'd tyek the jewel me-sel,
>   But really aw's not strang.
> There's flooer and coals te get,
>   The hoose-turns thor not deun;
> So haud the bairn for fairs,
>   Ye've often deun'd for fun.

Grudgingly Geordy agreed to 'haud the bairn for fairs' but his wife had not long been gone when he was heartily tired of the job. This all had a salutary effect on the 'Da' ' (which is the pitmatic for father), as he soon began to realize what a hard life his wife had.

Numerous verses go into details of Geordy's first unsuccessful efforts to keep the bairn quiet; by 'hikin't' up and down ('hike' according to Heslop is to toss up and down, and evidently Geordy was unable to 'kep' (catch it). At last peace is restored and in the final verse although still longing for his wife's return, Geordy says,

> But kindness does a vast,
>   It's ne use gettin' vext;
> It winnet please the bairn,
>   Or ease a mind perplexed.
> At last, it's gyen te sleep,
>   Me wife'll not say aw's num;
> She'll think aw's a real gud nurse—
>   Aw wish yor muther wad cum.

'Cappy, or The Pitman's Dog' by William Mitford, was originally written as a poem, and subsequently set to music. Again, this is typical, as in his own opinion any dog owned by a pitman is always endowed with every possible quality and sagacity. Cappy certainly must have been a most extraordinary animal.

It takes eleven verses to extol the wonders of this dog which lived near the City of Newcastle, and has a chorus repeated after each verse.

> In a toon near Newcastle a pitmen did dwell,
> Wiv his wife, nyem'd Peg, a tom-cat, and his sel.
> A dog called Cappy he doated upon,
> Because he was gi'en him by great-uncle Tom.
> Weel bred Cappy, Famous au'd Cappy;
> Cappy's the dog, Tallio, tallio.

Cappy had such amazing adventures, even being felled by a highwayman—which he happily survived. Perhaps the belief that a cat has nine lives was wrong for once and it was Cappy who was endowed with the proverbial number of lives.

Northumberland has every reason to be proud of its song and verse; they form part of the tangled history of the county. The Sailors, the Border raiders, the legendary figures, and last but by no means least in importance, the pitmen all have their share in folk songs in their own tongue.

Though not of the calibre of A. C. Swinburne, the county has also produced many minor poets. In some instances this verse could not be described as of a high standard, but practically without exception the great love which the Borderer has for his county is expressed in his attempts to sing its praises in verse.

One of these lovers of Northumberland wrote of his county in summer.

> O come with me by banks o' Tyne!
> Green banks beside a silver stream,
> Where sparkling, flashing, gleam on gleam,
> The sun-kissed waters swirl and shine,
> 'Neath shady trees, where some stray beam
> Of golden splendour pierces through
> 'Mid emerald leaf and diamond dew.
> Then upward from the stream again
> By a long, sweet, rose-scented lane,
> Where timid violets shyly peep,
> And trailing honeysuckles creep,
> And blackbirds trill their songs of love;
> Through the tall fir-wood, out and past
> A pleasant farm-stead, till at last
> We reach the open fells above.
> A golden haze of summer fell
> Stretches away on every hand,
> Hills bathed in purple distance stand,
> Like giants 'neath some fairy spell.
> A thousand birds sing clear and tell
> Tis summer time on Borderland!

'Plate' Day at Gosforth Park
The Tynedale Foxhounds against a background of Northumberland grass

13

Present Day Northumberland

Between our Eastward and our Westward sea,
The narrowing strand
Clasps close the noblest shore fame holds in fee,
Even here where English birth sets all men free—
Northumberland!
                              —Algernon Charles Swinburne

IN case any reader unfamiliar with Northumberland should gain the impression that such a historic county lives in the past, the writer felt that it was imperative to include a chapter on life in Northumberland today. Proud though Northumbrians are of their long history and incomparable scenery they are very much alive to the changes which are taking place, and in no way do they lag behind the times.

The writer has been asked so often when in the south of England what, if anything, happens in Northumberland, the question usually being "What do you do up there?" as though the county was cut off from all civilization! The fact is that there is often too much to do in Northumberland.

Several times in the press it has been reported that when a drive has been made to attract new industries to move to the North-east, that it is the wives of the workers who refuse to come. Under the impression that the county is bleak and isolated with little or no social life, they are hesitant to tear up their roots in the more gentle climate of the south.

When strangers do come to Northumberland to live, they are, with few exceptions, pleasantly surprised, not only by the warm welcome which they receive but by the number of activities in

L

The village of Etal

which they can take part. To enumerate a list of all that goes on in this Border county would cover pages. It is not only in the City of Newcastle and the market towns of the county where so many organizations flourish; the rural areas are also alive and progressive.

Northumberland has something to offer all tastes. It is one of the most sporting counties in the United Kingdom. Should anyone wish to hunt there are several packs to choose from, depending on where in the county one lives. In the Alnwick district it is The Percy, of which the Duke of Northumberland is Master. In this part of Northumberland too are The West Percy, The Milvain and The North Northumberland which runs to the Border. The College Valley hunts the hill foxes in the Cheviot country, while the appropriately named Border Hunt and the North Tyne takes in the wild moorlands of the Ottercops and Redesdale. The encroachment of the vast forests in this part of Northumberland have restricted both The Border and The North Tyne Hunts, and their country is smaller than it used to be. In South Tynedale it is The Haydon Hunt, largely a farmers' hunt which provides sport, and at the same time keeps the number of foxes under control, while the more fashionable Tynedale takes in a large tract of central Northumberland, and The Morpeth, as its name implies, lies within reach of that busy little town.

The Braes of Derwent hunts both in Northumberland and Durham south of the Tyne, and takes its name from the river which, for part of its course, forms a boundary between the two counties. Several of these hunts hold Point-to-Point Meetings in the spring, and nearly all have Hunt Balls in the winter some of which are held in the great houses of Northumberland. For example that of The Morpeth Hunt is held at Meldon, the home of Lieut-Colonel J. C. B. Cookson, and Alnwick Castle is the scene of The Percy's revelries which is one of the social events of the year in the county.

For those who prefer their sport on foot The Newcastle and District Beagles are extremely popular.

Racing is not neglected and until 1966 there were three courses. For some reason difficult to understand, the powers that be in far away London decided that The County of Northumberland Hunt Meeting at Rothbury should be abolished. Despite many angry protests against this unnecessary closure the stewards of The National Hunt Committee had their way, and now after two hundred years there is no racing in the green valley of the Coquet.

At Hexham in Tynedale the racecourse is on the heights of Yarridge south of the town, from which there are magnificent views to the south and north. There is no flat racing at Hexham, all its events being under National Hunt Rules. In the past there have been three two-day meetings in the year, with an occasional evening meeting. The Spring, The Whit and The Autumn meetings made up the calendar. Now that Whitsuntide is no longer a Bank Holiday, and a Spring Holiday has been substituted, there may have to be changes.

Gosforth Park, where the Newcastle race meetings are held, has racing both under Jockey Club and National Hunt rules. It is at Gosforth, in its beautiful surroundings, that the famous Northumberland Plate, locally known as 'The Pitman's Derby', is run. Vast changes have taken place at 'The Park' in the last four years and now its amenities compare favourably with the better known courses of the south. The Members' enclosure and Tattersall's are under cover, and as the Tote is under cover too, it is possible to go racing at Gosforth without ever going outside. Lifts are provided and the glass enclosed stands enable the racegoer to have an excellent view. From the top of the stands on a fine day it is a wonderful picture, with scarcely a sign of industry to be seen. Not only does racing take place at 'The Park', but there is an excellent golf course where international matches are played. Within the confines of Gosforth Park there is also a lake and a bird sanctuary. The new luxury hotel, named 'The Gosforth Park' is reached by an entrance from the Great North Road which leads to the racecourse. This Hotel was opened in October 1966 by the Duke of Northumberland. It fills a much needed gap since, if industry is to be persuaded to come to Tyneside there must be suitable accommodation for visitors and Newcastle has very few good hotels.

Racing is strongly supported not only by Northumbrians but from both sides of the Border, and trainers send their horses many miles to compete for some of the valuable prize money now to be won at 'The Park'. Many of the events are named after Northumbrian towns or villages such as the Rothbury Cup, a new innovation to take the place of the original which was run at the defunct County Meeting. Chesters Stakes take their name from the home of the late Captain A. M. Keith, whose filly, Frieze won the Oaks at Epsom in 1952.

Although hunting and racing are so popular in Northumberland there are many other forms of sport. There is fishing in the many rivers and streams, and in the little lakes north of the Roman Wall, Crag, Greenlee and Broomlee, while visitors to the 'Percy Arms' at Otterburn can fish in Sweethope Lough. In some of the reservoirs of the Newcastle and Gateshead Water Company special day tickets can be obtained to fish their waters, whilst the company's Catcleugh (in the Border country) and Colt Crag (which lies to the east of Watling Street) reservoirs are reserved for private fishing clubs. At the new Derwent Reservoir recently opened by Princess Alexandra, day tickets for fishing can be obtained, and there is also a sailing club.

Compared with Scotland and Yorkshire there are not so many shooting syndicates, most of the landowners and farmers shooting over their own land. There is a great deal of 'rough' shooting in Northumberland, as the writer knows from bitter experience, although not shooting herself, she has on occasions in the past 'beaten' near the Wall town and Alloa Lea. After these experiences (unpaid) it is obvious why the professional beaters, if they can be described as such, are well paid for their labours. The Glorious Twelfth can differ a great deal from the pictures in glossy magazines of glamorous looking females sitting on their shooting sticks beside the 'guns' in the butts. The peat bogs of the Roman Wall country are treacherous and the going hard, but nevertheless if one likes this form of exercise and there is a good bag at the end of the day, it is worth it all. Partridge and pheasant shoots are less arduous for the beaters although tramping through plough and beating the hedgerows and woodlands requires stamina.

Although these, which could be described as traditional country sports, are so popular there are many other ways of enjoying the exhilarating air of Northumberland. In the winter ski-ing has become very popular on the steep slopes at Allenheads and Allendale, and clubs have been formed. In other parts of the county winter sports are also popular, and when there is a hard winter there are many stretches of water where skaters can safely enjoy this form of sport. In Newcastle lakes in the municipal parks are popular with the town dwellers, and there is an indoor skating rink at Whitley Bay, which is extremely popular with the young people.

Some rock climbing can be done on the basalt cliffs which tower above Crag Lough, though of course not to such an extent as in Scotland and the Lake District.

The Cheviot range is a paradise for hill climbers, and for those who enjoy exploring the countryside on foot, Northumberland has countless walks of infinite variety, details of which can be obtained from The Ramblers' Association which has its headquarters in Newcastle. Armed with the appropriate ordnance maps the walker may spend many rewarding days following footpaths and byways which the motorist is unable to penetrate. Part of the longest footpath in Great Britain, The Pennine Way, passes through Northumberland. This Way has a course of 250 miles from where it begins in the Peak District of Derbyshire, until it ends its journey at Kirk Yetholm, just over the Border from Northumberland, in Roxburghshire. This now famous footpath is the result of proposals made by the National Parks Commission. It was a stupendous undertaking, as local authorities had to be consulted about new rights of way to join up with existing bridle tracks, pack horse and drove roads, tracks made by lead miners and shepherds, and in some cases, Roman roads; some grass grown, many of these being unmarked on the Ordnance maps. Even now there is no map which deals exclusively with the Way, but the National Parks Commission will gladly advise walkers which maps they should use. At Gilderdale where the burn of that name forms a boundary between Northumberland and Cumberland the Way crosses the burn and starts its long journey to the Border. By Gilsland and Greenhead along part of the Great Wall of Hadrian the walker can follow the Way. The journey is through some of the most awe inspiring and magnificent scenery in Northumberland. Fell land and forest, through uplands and lowlands the footpath leads the traveller on. By North Tyne and the valley of the Rede Water, by the lonely Byrness into the Cheviot country, and eventually climbing Cheviot itself.

Following The Pennine Way in any part of its course is a test of endurance, and should only be attempted by experienced walkers and those who love and understand the countryside, and have respect for other people's property. The Ramblers' Association warns those who contemplate following the Way, in any part of its course, but especially in Northumberland, to make arrangements for accommodation for the night well ahead, as there are many long miles between food and shelter. A delightful pictorial map has been issued by the Stationery Office, which though not drawn to scale, nevertheless gives a rough idea of the country through which the path makes its way. It is possible to borrow appropriate ordnance maps from The Ramblers' Association in London. The footpath's very name is romantic, and what an achievement it must be for anyone to be able to say, "I have walked The Pennine Way".

Although this chapter deals with the Northumberland of today it is impossible to avoid mentioning Northumberland's past, especially on The Pennine Way. Field-Marshal Viscount Montgomery of Alamein, when asked what was the value of history replied, "You have to learn from the past how to deal with the future". The walker from Gilderdale to Kirk Yetholm walks through history, much of it Roman, as the Way leads him to the top of Winshields Crag, the highest point to which the Wall climbs. From the Winshields the rest of the journey is largely through the country of the Border Raiders. The men of North Tyne and Rede Valley are descended from these reivers who lifted cattle and sheep from the backend to the spring, burning the Pele towers as they rode the foray, who helped to form the fabric of Northumbrian history and the Northumbrian character with its fierce independence and pride of family. Professor G. M. Trevelyan, in his *Social History of England* says, "There is less class distinction in Northumberland than in any other English county", which makes pleasant reading until this great historian gives his reasons; he goes on to say that practically every Northumbrian family was involved in 'lifting' his neighbours' stock; therefore we were all equally certain to have had an ancestor hanging from the gallow's tree! Not that any good Northumbrian is ashamed of his ancestor's exploits, in fact there is a tendency to brag that some of one's forebears paid the penalty of Jethart Justice, when a sheep stealer was hanged first and tried afterwards! Strangers venturing along the Northumbrian stretch of The Pennine Way today need have no fear; the Northumbrian is a reformed character.

Now in North Tyne and Redesdale where Robsons, Dodds, Milburns, Charltons and many more Borderers rounded up the cattle and sheep, are the thousands of acres of trees planted by the Forestry Commission. Instead of the sheep which succeeded the raiders after the days of the Union roe deer have multiplied, especially in the vast forest of Kielder. The Commission does its best to keep the numbers under control, as deer can do so much damage. These gentle looking creatures are capable of creating havoc both to trees and agricultural land.

To keep the numbers under control, there is, in the open season a fair amount of stalking under the strict supervision of the Commission. Only expert shots are allowed to take part in these stalks so that needless cruelty can be avoided. Recently one day permits have been granted, again only to proved marksmen, and a new sport can thus be enjoyed in Northumberland. The stalkers are accompanied by one of the Forestry Commission keepers. The object is to improve the herd and see that any weakly bucks are destroyed before the mating season.

Red deer, unlike the roe are creatures of the uplands and are rarely found in the woodlands, although there has been evidence from time to time that a stag has visited Kielder Forest and has actually been seen. The Stationery Office has issued an excellent handbook on the National Forests, called *Border Guide*, which deals with the various aspects of life in the Forests. Not only does it describe the land and the people, but includes interesting chapters on local history, wild life and geology, to mention only a few subjects. The Northumberland National Park also has a handbook, which although not so comprehensive contains a great deal of useful information.

Could the Border raiders return to their 'Country' now they would fail to recognize it, and in the words of the late Howard Pease, from one of his many poems on Northumberland:

No more across the moors in rout,
The redshank Scots shall fly;
No more our raiding horse pursue,
Like hounds upon the cry.

Northumberland has seen many changes throughout the centuries, but it can be truly said it has marched with the times and not lived on its past.

Not only can these 'inland' sports be enjoyed, there is much to do on the Northumbrian coast. Since the war sailing has increased in popularity, and there are several sailing clubs. The headquarters of the Royal Northumberland Yacht Club is at Blyth, which is not particularly attractive but has a good harbour. Until a short time ago Blyth was a flourishing town, but with the closure of the shipyard it is threatened with a high rate of unemployment.

Collingwood's memorial at Tynemouth looks down on the many little boats which lie alongside the pier, and further up the coast at Beadnell and Seahouses amateur sailors enjoy their sailing at weekends. Changes take place so rapidly that by the time this book is in print Northumberland may have added even more attractions to its long list.

Far away from the little ships and the coast, at Corbridge on the Tyne, there is a scheme to have an indoor riding school, and so encourage show jumping of a high standard. A committee was formed by the late Sir Douglas Blackett of Halton Castle, and if there is enough support it is proposed to build the school on the Tyneside Agricultural Society's permanent show field at Corbridge. This long established show was once a one-day event, but with the changes in the national holidays it was held in 1967 on the Spring Holiday and again at the end of August. In 1968 the Society reverted to a one-day show.

These are only some of the outdoor sports which can be enjoyed. There are several good golf clubs both near Newcastle and in the country. A County Tennis Tournament is held every year in Jesmond and although cricket is not worshipped as it is in Yorkshire, county matches are played, and many of the villages and market towns have clubs.

Although Northumberland has so much to offer in sporting and outdoor recreations, there is also, to use an overworked word, a cultural side, which has a formidable list of societies both within the city boundaries of Newcastle and in the rural areas.

A directory of societies issued by the City Information Service lists nine subjects all of which are sub-divided into various sections. Dancing figures prominently in the list, which includes the Newcastle Morris Men. This group is for the purpose of keeping alive the traditional dances, especially the Tyneside Rapper and the Long Sword dancing. At intervals the Morris Men, wearing their picturesque costume, visit towns and villages in the County and give open-air displays. The Northumberland Barn Dance Club favours Scottish Country dancing, and they too, extend their activities beyond the city boundaries. In spite of the impact of television there are amateur dramatic and operatic societies which flourish in various parts of Northumberland. It is regrettable that the 'live' theatre in Newcastle has become a victim of the changing times, and apart from the Peoples' Theatre which attracts a regular clientele, the two other theatres, the Royal in Newcastle's most imposing thoroughfare Grey Street, and the Flora Robson Playhouse, named in honour of the celebrated actress who has close connections with Tyneside, are both under threat of closure. There is a cloud hanging over the Old Assembly Rooms in Westgate Road, one of the few Georgian buildings which has not been demolished in the doubtful name of progress, a word now which covers a multitude of sins. For nearly two hundred years the most important functions in Newcastle have been held in these Rooms. Royal visitors to the North East have dined and danced under the crystal chandeliers from the days of candlelight to the present time. The last Royal visitor was H.R.H. Princess Margaret Countess of Snowdon.

In contrast to the decline of the 'live' theatre and the threat to historic buildings, there has been an intense revival of interest in local history. This is a peculiar trait in the British character that when there is a danger of the disappearance of the old and familiar every effort is made to keep it! Only too often the protests are too late, and when there is a conducted tour of the historic buildings of old Newcastle (and there are several) it is nostalgic to hear remarks such as "This is where once were part of the city walls".

In the country districts there are several societies which study local history, from Berwick to Hexham, at Rothbury the capital of Coquetdale, to mention only a few; these societies are strongly supported.

Although abreast of the times the born and bred Northumbrian is intensely interested in the events which have taken place in his county and there is still a great deal of local pride taken in 'our town' or 'our village'. In spite of the infiltration of 'foreigners' and the many means of travel which are available today, a 'real' Northumbrian is convinced there is nothing anywhere comparable with this comparatively unknown County, an opinion which the writer unashamedly shares!

There is an excellent Reference Library in Newcastle's New Bridge Street, and the County Archivists are always ready to answer queries. It is in The Archivist's Office in Melton Park, that many of the personal papers and records of Northumberland's ancient families have been deposited for safe keeping. Melton Park is situated on the east side of the Great North Road and is one of the many new and attractive housing estates which have been built in recent years.

In the city itself is the Literary and Philosophical Society. Not only has this Society a magnificent collection of books but a series of lectures is held in the winter months, and these cover a wide variety of subjects. The County Library at Morpeth also has a special section devoted to local history.

Naturally there is a Society of Antiquaries, who not only hold meetings at regular intervals but make excursions into the counties of both Northumberland and Durham to visit places of historic interest.

Musical societies flourish as is to be expected in the only English county where pipes are played—the Northumbrian pipes; these sweet sounding small pipes which differ from the Scottish as they are operated by an arm bellow and not 'wind blown'. There is a Society of Pipers, which gives its aims as "To keep alive and extend interest in the making and playing of Northumbrian Pipes, and especially to encourage young players". An old couplet expresses the aims in a more romantic way:

> Still linger in our northern clime
> Some remnants of the good old time.

The origin of the Northumbrian pipes has never been explained, though their construction, if that is the right word, is known to have changed over the centuries; for example, the pipes which are played today are different from those of over a hundred years ago. It is difficult today to find many pipe makers but in bygone times there were several men employed in making this instrument which is uniquely Northumbrian. The skill in playing the pipes has often been handed down from father to son, and such families were spoken of as 'piping' families.

Today the pipes are a relic of the past which has happily survived but at one time they were part of the pattern of Northumbrian life and were played at all the local gatherings, sometimes even in church! In 1933 some interesting articles appeared in the local press and extracts are well worth quoting. There was a "J. Dunn of Newcastle, the Halls of Hedgely, and Robert and James Reid of North Shields. It was these Reids who, by their scientific skill, increased the keys on the chanter to seventeen, and the drones to six in number . . . in North-West Northumberland noted performers on the small pipes were the Armstrongs of Linacres, and Warksburn. Descendants of these same Armstrongs [presumably the writer is referring to 1933] are still living at Raylees, Otterburn, and still piping" . . . the anonymous writer then goes on to say that four years ago (that would be in 1929) he had a letter from the late Mr John Errington of Carlisle, who wrote "Seventy years ago I was staying with my Uncle at The Haining at the head of Warksburn, when Mr John Armstrong of Hindley Steel and his brother (a fiddler and piper) came to the Haining and spent the evening, and I well remember their performance on the pipes which I heard for the first time . . ." Then there were the Bateys and the Charltons of North Tyne . . . the Gray family of Prudhoe and Ovington were well known pipers eighty years ago . . . among others the Clough family of Newsham is mentioned and many others held the position which Jack Armstrong does today as that of Piper to The Duke of Northumberland. In this sophisticated day and age of pop music, it is remarkable that piping still survives, and that the art is still practised in the Northumberland of today, another instance of how traditions die hard in spite of the changes which are taking place daily in the hectic rat race of the 1960s.

Not only does tradition survive but old customs have in many cases managed to withstand the realistic attitude of the youth of today. In some rural areas of Northumberland Hallow E'en is still celebrated. 'Dooking' (ducking) for apples is one, and some children make lanterns out of a hollow turnip; two holes representing the eyes, a mouth and a nose are carved and the lighted candle placed inside the turnip shell, a handle of string is attached and these turnip lanterns have a terrifying appearance when carried swinging through the dark.

In industrial Northumberland, especially in the coalfield, where more and more miners are compelled to change their way of life completely as the collieries close and the 'new' towns spring up, some traditions and superstitions linger on. It will be interesting to see how quickly the social structure changes, as in every sense of its meaning the mining community has always been a closed shop.

Bingo has superseded the quoit matches, but the miner has the old affection for his brass bands. The 'Telly' rules the household as at one time did the whippet, a thin and smaller edition of the greyhound, but the pitman of Northumberland still indulges in his love of racing pigeons. He and 'the wife' now go to foreign parts for their holidays but the great events of the year still take place in his own county. In the autumn it is the leek shows which draw the crowds. These vegetables are treasured like the Crown Jewels, and grow to the most gigantic sizes; the amount of prize money offered for competition at the shows is often £500 or more.

The Working Men's Clubs in some of the villages are palatial but have long since lost their original purpose which was educational. Vast quantities of beer ('best Scotch') are consumed at the Club, but there is no one more generous a giver than a pitman. Outings are organized for old people and children, and when he has something left in the pay-packet no appeal for charity is ignored.

Northumberland is indeed a county of contrasts in its scenery as well as its people. No two people could be more different than a shepherd in the Cheviot country and the pitman from Ashington or any other part of the coalfield. The many superstitions which have been observed for so long are possibly the outcome of a dangerous way of life, especially in the Northumberland coalfield with its memories of the Hartley Pit disaster. At one time a pitman on his way to work would turn back if he met a woman wearing a white apron, believing that she was an omen of death. The origin of this unusual superstition was that in every colliery village at one time, there was a woman who acted as official 'layer-out' and whoever was engaged in this macabre occupation always wore a white apron! There is no doubt that now, with a higher standard of living and the educational facilities denied to their forefathers, these beliefs will gradually die out.

It is quite impossible to enumerate all the different activities that take place in Northumberland, such an attempt would read like Forthcoming Events in Britain! There is something to appeal to all. There are the arts, sport, enjoyment of the ever changing scenery, a study of the colourful history of England's most exciting and 'genuine' county or, for those who enjoy it, the night life of Tyneside in the numerous night clubs which appear to have such a strong appeal to some people.

In spite of this invasion from other parts of the country the

Northumbrian is always ready to accept new ways provided he is getting a square deal. It must be admitted that there is still a certain amount of feudalism, especially in the country districts.

This attempt to paint a word picture of Northumberland today, is seen through the eyes of a Northumbrian. Strangers may gain a very different impression; but as the Norsemen came long ago to ravage the Kingdom of Northumbria and then settled in, to them, a foreign land, so the invader of today soon settles in the county of his adoption. In some cases he becomes more pro-Northumbrian than the genuine article!

14

The Road to Cornhill

O, you'll take the high road,
And I'll take the low road,
And I'll be in Scotland afore ye.
—from the Morven Collection of Scottish Songs

THIS book begins with the story of a road, the A1, and it ends by following the course of another highway which leads to Scotland, the A697 as it is prosaically numbered.

Leaving the Great North Road at Northgate about two miles beyond the town of Morpeth, the traveller who chooses this route to the Border passes through some of the most dramatic and beautiful scenery in Northumberland. In its long journey to the Tweed, which until near the end of its course divides the two countries, the road passes through purely agricultural land. The only sign of industry is the brick works at Swarland.

Northumberland is so fortunate in, up to now, being one of the few counties left which have not become urbanized. Compared with many other parts of England where the countryside is fast disappearing to make way for factories and the ugliness which results, Northumberland's industrial area is all in one corner.

Though not so famous as the Great North Road, this highway is steeped in history, and the many byways which branch off to the east and west lead to hamlets, great houses and farmsteads which all have their individual stories. It is a road that beckons, for in the far distance the Cheviot Range gives the impression of waiting for the traveller to reach the foothills, and wander through the many valleys, which lead to the heights of this geographical barrier between England and Scotland. The Cheviot hills on a sunny day resemble the mountains in the psalm which 'skipped like young lambs', but when the clouds are low the Muckle Cheviot wears its cap, and 'glowers' over the vast expanse of scenery.

Any road which leads to a Border has a certain romance, and the most famous song ever written about a road is 'Loch Lomond' Many are the theories and versions concerning the high and low roads, but as all are based on legend it is impossible to vouch for the factual truth of any. Some say that the song writer, who is unknown, was inspired by an episode in the Rebellion of the 'Forty-five' and that the man who 'reached Scotland afore ye' was a survivor of this tragic attempt by Charles Edward Stuart to restore his dynasty, while the other man died on English soil, and that it was his spirit that returned to Scotland by the 'low' road. There is an old belief that the spirit of every Scot, who dies away from his own country, returns to Scotland by the 'low' road—which is a beautiful idea. A suggestion has been made that the words were written long after the music, and that Ben Jonson was responsible, but this is pure conjecture.

Whatever its origin this song is so appropriate for this road to Cornhill, as it is the quickest route of the many Northumbrian roads which lead to Scotland, if the starting point is from Northgate.

When Northgate is left behind, the scenery at first is rich and well wooded, gradually merging into moorland. Thousands of acres of grazing-land support the stock, which in this part of the county is so numerous. Few and far between are the villages on this undulating road; Longhorsley, Longframlington, Powburn, and Milfield which is north of the town of Wooler, are the largest until Cornhill is reached.

In their different ways these villages are all worth exploring. The church at Longhorsley stands in a field away from the village—why this is so has never been explained; possibly the road like so many others has changed its course, as the little church of St Helen, although drastically restored was originally Norman. In those days the road would only be a track and would probably

Cheviot country: a one-time gamekeeper's cottage

be there before the village. Longhorsley has a Pele tower in an excellent state of preservation. Once the property of the Horsley family, from which the village obviously took its name, the 'long' also is most appropriate as the houses are strung out on both sides of the highway and give the appearance of a long village. A public house in the village has the unusual name of 'The Shoulder of Mutton'.

In summer when the hedgerows are ablaze with wild roses, which flourish profusely in this part of Northumberland, the scenery is at its most beautiful. The Simonside range lends a dramatic background as its stands guard over Coquetdale.

At the foot of the steep descent to Weldon Bridge, where a road branches off on its way to Rothbury by way of Pauperhaugh and the romantically situated Brinkburn Priory which has now been taken over by the Ministry of Works, stands the famous fishing inn, 'The Angler's Arms'. The old bridge which spans Coquet here has been the scene of so many accidents, and has been so severly damaged on many occasions, that a new bridge is now in the course of construction. This will eventually join up with a new road and so avoid the steep climb up the hill which is one in twelve.

Soon the village of Longframlington is reached, another 'long' village, and the character of the scenery is again changing. Earthworks abound in the Longframlington district, one being the curiously named Canada Camp.

There are many legends connected with the surrounding countryside, especially with Rimside Moor, once the haunt of highwaymen who were the terror of travellers. Rimside is bleak and brooding even today, and one can well believe the old ballad of 'The Black Sow of Rimside and the Monk of Holy Island,' which accounts for the old saying; "If ye were on Rimside Moor at twelve o'clock at night wi' a black sow by the tail, ye wadna' be here tonight".

Close to the road to Cornhill, in this part of its course near Longframlington, runs the Roman Devil's Causeway which can be traced with the help of an Ordnance map. On some of the old maps the Devil's Causeway is defined as Watling Street!

M

Border scenery

Northumbrians are determined to have a share in this most famous of Roman roads, regardless of its geographical position!

The scenery is now enchanting, little burns trickle down the hills which rise on every side; and to the west are Thrunton Crags, thickly planted with fir trees. This was the first of the Forestry Commission's plantations in Northumberland.

Suddenly, as so often happens in this county of infinite variety, the whole picture changes and the road makes a sharp descent to Bridge of Aln, where there is a hotel of that name. Here at the cross roads, the traveller can leave the main road and take the road leading to the delightful village of Whittingham, in the Vale of that name, and from there visit Callaly Castle (now open to the public), which stands on 'the Shepherd's brae'. On the way to Callaly is Eslington, the home of Lord Ravensworth.

Returning to the main road by way of Glanton, which overlooks the Vale of Whittingham, the traveller can make his way back to Bridge of Aln and take the moorland road to Alnwick, from which can be seen some of the most magnificent views in all Northumberland.

Yet it is the Cheviots which persistently beckon one to reach their foothills. In the words of Will Ogilvie:

> But before you win your welcome where the high tops wait
> You must make your bow to Cheviot as the guardian of the gate.

Whereas the Great North Road is a restless stretch of highway the road that leads to Cornhill is a beckoning road, urging the traveller ever onwards towards the Border and the Tweed. Yet to appreciate the beauties and assimilate the history of the many places of interest on the way, Cheviot must wait to welcome those who are making their way towards 'the guardian of the gate'.

From Bridge of Aln to Powburn long stretches of the road are so thickly lined with trees, that one gains the impression of being in a long green tunnel. Here, beside the road, at one time, was the track of the railway, now like so many other branch lines, abandoned. Many of the stationmasters' former houses and waiting rooms have been converted into dwellings, and some of them are quite delightful. The railway station at Powburn is Hedgeley, so called because the 'big' house here is Hedgeley Hall, the home of the Carr-Ellison family.

The inn at Powburn is 'The Plough'. Here in the days when coaches were the chief means of transport, 'The Plough' was a house of call, and the present occupier has many interesting records of those days. The road of the coaching days approached Powburn from a different direction from its route today, possibly to avoid some of the many steep hills. 'The Red Rover' coach to Newcastle called at 'The Plough' on its way 'from The Waterloo Hotel' in Edinburgh. There have been many changes at 'The Plough' since the days of the 'Red Rover', and several of them in comparatively recent times. It is fascinating to read the account books which were kept at the beginning of this century, and when the prices are compared with those of the present time, it is understandable why elderly people refer to 'the good old days'. There is a bill at 'The Plough' to one of the local gentry for wines and spirits. Thirteen bottles of whisky came to £2 8s. 9d., while twelve bottles of hock cost 3s. No wonder many of our ancestors were 'three bottle men'. Bed and breakfasts prices were half a crown a night!

Leaving Powburn with nostalgic thoughts of days gone by, the twentieth-century traveller continues towards the Border, and crosses the river Breamish. Here the Cheviots appear in all their magnificence, not only a geographical but a political barrier between England and Scotland.

It is quite beyond the powers of any writer to describe the glorious view as the road goes on its way to Wooler. The rich farm lands, which gradually merge into moorland, the feeling of grandeur and freedom are impossible to express. This is peaceful Cheviot country, which it is difficult to believe once was fought over so bitterly. Scotsmen and Englishmen died in these now green fields. The Battle of Hedgeley Moor recalls the memory of a Percy, one of the many of his race, who fell fighting in the days of ceaseless warfare. There is a cross still standing a few miles to the north of Powburn which is known as Percy's Cross. This marks the spot where there was once a well, and tradition says that the dying man dragged himself there to quench his thirst. The Cross is difficult to find today as it stands behind a house on the roadside.

Before Wooler is reached the road passes the entrance leading to Lilburn Tower, the home of Sir Edward Collingwood. Here the scenery is softer, and a burn adds to the charm of the surroundings.

Wooler is the capital of Glendale as this part of Northumberland is called, taking its name from the river Glen, which joins the Till at Bewick Mill. Wooler is surrounded by hills and then suddenly a great plain spreads out, a result of a glacier long ago. Here on this plain is Milfield, where once General Monk encamped with an army which eventually became one of the most famous of all British Regiments, the Coldstream Guards. It is a far cry from the Glorious Restoration, which Monk's soldiers did so much to bring about, to the Second World War when there was an R.A.F. station at Milfield. This airfield is still operational for civilian flights.

From Milfield to the end of its journey the road is even more deeply steeped in history. From it can be seen the great castle of Ford, where King Jamie spent the night before Flodden. Many are the sign posts which point the way to Flodden Field, and the memorial "To the brave of both Nations" on Branxton Hill is an outstanding landmark.

> Dool and wae was the order sent our lads to the Border,
> The English for aince by guile won the day,
> The flowers of the forest that fought aye the foremost,
> The prime of our land are cold in the clay.

So lamented Jane Elliot in her incomparable ballad "The Flowers of the Forest".

Not so far from Ford is Etal, another of the many historic and picturesque villages which are tucked away from the hustle and bustle of present day life, and yet in so many ways are forging ahead in their progressive farming and estate management. Here is the property of Lord Joicey who is one of the biggest landowners in North Northumberland, and who practises the most modern and up to date methods on his estates.

The white 'harled' Fenton House is another outstanding landmark, and is one of the homes of Viscount Lambton, the Earl of Durham's heir and the member of Parliament for Berwick upon Tweed. Fenton House can be seen for miles, set in parkland, which overlooks the river Till as it meanders on its way to join the Tweed at Tillmouth.

At Fenton in the spring the North Northumberland Hunt, of which Lord Joicey is Joint Master, hold their Horse Trials, which attract entries from both England and Scotland. In fact these trials are rapidly becoming the 'Badminton' of the North.

Interesting and beautiful as are so many places on the road to Cornhill, Cheviot is beckoning impatiently, as though jealous of any rivals.

James Service a local poet born in the village of Chatton, had, like many poets, a chequered career. He endured hardship and poverty, and towards the end of his life was an inmate of the workhouse at Sunderland in County Durham. How this early nineteenth-century schoolmaster came to such dismal surroundings as a workhouse is not known, but his love for his native county and particularly of the Cheviot country never faltered.

> No more I gaze upon my native Cheviot's peaks
> Breaking the soft blue of the summer sky

wrote this pathetic old man, and another verse in praise of Northumberland is:

> O'er all thy wilds from Tweed's remotest verge
> To where the Tyne rolls blithe to ocean's surge
> No son of thine, how rude so e'er his heart,
> But feels it swell at what thou wast and art!

Poor James Service, long ago forgotten, yet his pathetic attempts at poetry have survived.

Before Cornhill is reached the roads branch off into the Cheviot valleys, and "the guardian of the gate" has his way at last. One of the most lovely valleys, though not so well known as the more famous College Valley, is the Valley of the Bowmont Water, a 'water' which joins the College Burn.

The hills rise steeply from the banks of Bowmont, and are

studded with small plantations of trees which add beauty to the landscape. Bowmont Water rises beyond the Scottish border and follows a winding course. The sturdy Cheviot sheep seem to cling to the precipitous slopes, and in the spring when they have been 'clipped', as Northumbrians call shearing, they stand out sharply, especially in the early evening, when the sun is setting. At Howtel there is a nature conservancy, and the Women's Insitute hold their meetings in what was once the school for this remote valley.

The end of the journey is near and at last Cornhill-on-Tweed, to give it the proper title, is reached. Cornhill, as its name implies, was a gathering place for the grain which was, and still is, extensively grown in this part of Northumberland. It is a delightful village, the last before the Tweed divides the two countries. To make matters more confusing to the stranger in Northumberland, the village, though in England and having its own Post Office (surely one of the smallest in the country) is for some unknown reason regarded by the G.P.O. as being in Scotland, as the postmark on the letters is Coldstream!

One of Northumberland's best hotels is at Cornhill, the appropriately named 'Collingwood Arms', as this famous family had and still have close connections with the district. The coloured inn sign is a picture of the late John Collingwood, who was always referred to as 'The Squire'. The Inn still retains its offer of 'Post Horses' in large lettering.

It has been impossible to discover exactly how old this house is; certainly it was there before 1865, as there is a photograph of it at this date in the hotel today, and judging from its appearance, it was then an old house; possibly it dates from the eighteenth century. Where the village shop is today there was once another inn, 'The Wagon'.

The church at Cornhill is modern by Northumbrian standards as it only dates from 1840, though the trees in the churchyard are much older. Prior to the building of the present church there was an ancient chapel of ease on this site.

In the church are many memorials to the Collingwood family.

A drive leads to Cornhill House, the home of Lieutenant-Colonel J. H. F. Collingwood who is a member of the senior branch of this very old family. The house stands in a delightful position, high above Tweed, which forms a loop here. Possibly Cornhill House was once a fortified dwelling as this part of the Border was always under threat of attack from their neighbours on the north side of Tweed. When peace at long last came, a farm-house was added to the original Pele tower and with later addi-tions became a country house. The view from the front door embraces a variety of beauty of great charm, with the Cheviots as a background. The line of the Border is such that though one is looking south here over Tweed the prospect is in Scotland!

An unusual picture in the possession of Colonel Collingwood is that of an ox which was roasted whole to celebrate the coming of age of a Collingwood of Lilburn in 1832. This enormous animal weighed one hundred stones, and the tallow, twenty stones. What a quantity of candles there must have blazed at Lilburn!

Regretfully leaving Cornhill behind, the road within Northum-berland is coming to an end. Presently the county sign is replaced after crossing Coldstream bridge by the Scottish sign, and looking back on to the glorious vista that is Northumberland is to make a Northumbrian prouder than ever of his county.

It seems appropriate to end this story of a county with a prayer in memory of Flodden. It is long since Northumberland was a battlefield and here on the Border, Scots and Englishmen are good friends and neighbours.

The Flodden Prayer

O Lord Jesus Christ who didst stretch forth Thine arms upon the Cross, to draw all men to Thyself, we beseech Thee that, as Thou hast given peace to the peoples of our own land, so Thou wilt give peace to all nations, and to the homes and hearts of all who dwell on earth, for Thy Holy Name's sake. Amen.

Index